Rules of
Engagement

Rules of Engagement

Building a Workplace Culture to Thrive in an Uncertain World

Carolyn Swora

CEO, Pinnacle Culture

BRIGHTFLAME
Books By Experts

For information, visit www.pinnacleculture.ca.

"PURPOSEFUL WORKPLACE EXPERIENCE" is a trademark owned by Carolyn Swora and no use of the mark is authorized without a licence.

Published in Canada by BrightFlame Books, Burlington, ON.

Do you have an authority book inside you?
www.brightflamebooks.com/getpublished

First Edition © 2018 Carolyn Swora.

ISBN (Paperback): 978-1-988179-35-3
ISBN (Hardback): 978-1-988179-36-0
ISBN (Ebook): 978-1-988179-37-7

Contents

Disclaimer

The publisher and author make no representations or warranties with respect to the accuracy or completeness of the contents of this work, including, and without limitation, warranties of fitness for a particular purpose. No warranty may be created or suitable for every situation.

Nothing in this work is a promise or guarantee of earnings. The content, case studies, and examples shared in this work should not be assumed to represent in any way "average" or "typical" results. Neither the author nor the publisher is familiar with you, your business, your market or your circumstances. Therefore, the case studies we are sharing can neither represent nor guarantee the current or future experience of other past, current or future clients. Rather these case studies and examples represent what is possible by applying the strategies presented.

Each of these examples is the culmination of numerous factors, many of which we cannot control, including pricing, market conditions, product or service quality, offer, customer service, personal initiative, and countless other variables, tangible and intangible. Your level of success in attaining results is dependent on many factors, including your skill, knowledge, experience, ability, connections, dedication, focus, business savvy and financial situation. Because these factors vary from individual to individual, we cannot guarantee your success or ability to earn revenue.

You alone are responsible for your actions and results in business and life, and in your use of these materials, you agree not to hold us liable for any of your decisions, actions or results, at any time, or under any circumstances.

No portion of this work is intended to offer legal, medical, personal or financial advice. If professional assistance is required, the services of a competent professional should be sought. Neither the publisher nor the author shall be liable for damages arising herefrom.

Under no circumstances, including but not limited to negligence, will the author or publisher, or any of their representatives or contractors be held liable for any special or consequential damages that result from the use of, or inability to use, the materials, information, or success strategies communicated through this work, or any services following this work, even if advised of the possibility of such damages.

The fact that an organization, individual or website is referred to as a source of further information does not mean that the author or the publisher endorses the information the organization or website may provide, or recommendations it may make. Further, readers should be aware that internet websites listed in this work may have changed or disappeared between when this work was written and when it was read.

In other words, nothing in this book should be taken as any form of contractual obligation. Neither the author, her company, the publishers, nor their assignees warrant any result from implementing the ideas in this book, and they accept no liability for any damage, loss or harm to you or any third party arising from any interpretation or implementation of the ideas in this book. *Caveat lector (reader beware)*.

Register This Book

As a thank you for buying this book I'd like to give you some free resources.

Simply visit

http://pinnacleculture.ca/bookregistration/

and confirm your purchase to get access to an infographic of my book and helpful videos.

Foreword

Why Is It Hard for So Many?

by Dan Pontefract, Bestselling author of Flat Army and The Purpose Effect

On one hand, you have leaders—strapped to a meteorite of scientific management principles—who seem not to care that their employee base is disengaged, even disaffected. In fact, they are contributing to such a predicament. On the other hand, there are those employees who wander aimlessly from task-to-task and job-to-job betting on lottery tickets called "hopes and wishes" for better fortunes.

This was not how things were supposed to be. This is not the meaningful workplace we had hoped for.

When we arrive at an organization to begin a new role—be it as a leader or a team member—we have certain expectations. Civility, kind heartedness, collaborative people, interesting work and opportunities for growth are but a few of the attributes we look forward to. Some would call these table stakes, like condiments at a beach barbecue.

All too often something unfortunate happens. Employees get sucked into a vortex of workplace meaningless. The culture might be very rigid, rife with fiefdoms and silos. Team members refuse to collaborate with one another. Fear and angst is rampant. Doing what's right becomes an exercise in keeping our heads down for fear of reprisal. What we signed up for is the opposite of what we are experiencing.

Sometimes the organization and its leaders have enacted and then enabled a corporate culture—and operating ethos—that runs counter to your own values. Perhaps its only motive is to hike margins and to increase levels of profitability. You ask yourself, "What about our community, the environment, or society?" Those questions fall on deaf ears.

Sometimes the culture is one where command and control leadership suffocates any chance for more meaningful work, innovative ideas, or collaborative partnerships. Perhaps the stifling bureaucracy that is upheld by leaders across the organization is causing irreparable harm to not only your work, but customer satisfaction levels. All of it is deeply concerning to you. There has to be a better way.

There *is* a better way. I believe it is called *purpose*.

An individual who seeks a sense of purpose in their workplace will be one who is constantly developing, defining and deciding their values, priorities, attributes and general ways of conducting themselves in their activities. It is a perpetual cycle of self-discovery. When we lose sight of our purpose—when we give in to the organization's lack of purpose—there is no doubt in my mind that it affects the core of our soul.

In Carolyn's book, she encourages us to seek out, develop, define and decide our purpose as it relates to being part of—and indeed establishing—a meaningful workplace. "Everyone is a leader," she correctly observes, and as she deftly and persuasively argues throughout the following pages, it is up to us as team members and leaders to create such a sense of purpose. That is for ourselves, the people we work with, and the organization that employs us.

It is no longer good enough to consent to yesterday's archaic organizational practices as the standard for tomorrow's needs. We cannot accept to work in an organization or in a role that lacks purpose. A new form of purpose-driven leadership is required. Instead of making it hard, let's make it easy, for the many. The pages that follow do not disappoint.

Preface

Workplace Disrupted

The concept of disruption has permeated our world over the last few years. *Disruption* is the idea that how we behave and operate changes drastically. We constantly hear how our lives are being "disrupted" by things like smartphones and AI. For many of us, the workplace is an integral part of our lives, and it too is being disrupted.

Disrupt has a negative feel to it, however. I prefer to use the word *evolve*.

One of the major evolutions you are probably already experiencing is the shift toward team-based projects, also called *cross-functional teams* or *matrixed teams*.

The key to the future success of companies is how well networks of teams operate together. In the future, teams will form quickly, and disband once the project is complete. Your success will depend (if it doesn't already) on relationships and how well you can build networks to get things done. The speed at which you are able to do this authentically will be a key success factor.

The modern organization is no longer a hierarchy, where your only direct connections are to the person above or below you. Organizations are switching to a matrix structure to make themselves more flexible in responding to the conflicting needs of the market and internal stakeholders—as many as 84% of organizations according to research by McKinsey & Co.[1]

I wrote this book for CEOs, leaders, and managers who see their business environment changing rapidly around them; who suddenly find themselves fighting the pressures of volatility, uncertainty, complexity, and ambiguity—forces which I refer to by the acronym VUCA throughout this book because they have become such a constant feature of business life that they merit having their own name.

My hope is that this book will evolve your thinking and challenge you to reflect on "how" your company operates. I hope it will be a call to action for you and that you will realize you are not alone. The workplace is being disrupted, and we need to embrace new ways of working. We need to evolve.

More importantly, I want you to understand that there are steps you can take to meet those challenges.

Too many managers rely on hope as a management technique.

They sit at their desk, watching the pressure mount, and hope that things will eventually calm down: all they have to do is weather the storm until it happens. The problem is, the world outside is not going to stop changing, and—almost without exception—the changes that happen do not go away, and they don't reverse, so you need to adapt. You need to change your own approach.

They hope that they—and their employees—will find ways to use technology to make themselves more productive. The

---

[1] McKinsey Quarterly, Revisiting the matrix organization, 2016.

problem is, as we will see in Part One of the book, it's technology that's creating the problem in the first place.

It's not about time management and productivity tools anymore. It's about different skill sets, and learning how to deal with what's happening and adapt.

As you read this book, my intent is that you will realize that, while it may feel like the world is spinning out of control, you actually have control over a lot more than you think you do. The key to dealing with VUCA is to focus on those things that you do control.

Ultimately, the core message of this book is simple. We can make a lot more money in business, and be more efficient if we let go of outmoded models of thinking that treat organizations—and people—like machines.

You have to be willing to let go of traditional notions of management and leadership. One day, we may not even see individuals with management titles. We don't need managers anymore. We need leaders who understand both how business works *and* how people work.

Carolyn Swora
Burlington, Ontario, Canada

Introduction

The Long Road to Purpose

The idea of this book was born at a time in my life when the Universe threw everything it had at me.

It started on the day the doctor dropped the bombshell.

For several months, my husband, Paul, had been complaining about not feeling great. He was always tired. He'd lost his appetite. There was the constant, nagging back pain. Then one day there was blood in his urine, and that was what sent him to the doctor.

We'd thought it would be stress, or overwork, or any one of a number of easy-to-fix annoyances of modern working life. What we weren't prepared for was stage 4 renal carcinoma—kidney cancer.

It was 2003, and we had been married just over a year. Suddenly, I had a full-time responsibility at home alongside my full-time responsibilities at work. And, oh yes, I was expecting our first son.

I joined an international pharmaceutical company in 1999 and, for four years, my career had followed the standard employee journey at the company. I was a manager, doing what managers do: getting on with my work, and getting things done.

Virtually overnight, life became a blur of medical appointments, hard conversations with family and friends, and even harder conversations at home. We were also making trips to the US so Paul could get treatment that wasn't available in Canada.

Our first son, Ayden, was born four months after Paul's diagnosis. So, now, I added being a new mother to the list of responsibilities and challenges I was dealing with.

Despite all of that—and even with the birth of our second son Andrew eighteen months later—I continued to function at work. Or so I thought, at least.

My career progressed, and I was growing a reputation for building successful teams in an industry that was constantly changing, and in a highly pressurized business environment. All while navigating a life-changing experience at home.

That story forms the backdrop of this book, so I won't go into it in detail here. But the skills I developed in that period became invaluable and got me through the chaos, not just at home, but at work.

Why you need to read this book

Look around your office. Statistically, for every ten people you see, six of them are feeling overwhelmed[2], and that particular statistic is only going to become worse as time goes on.

---

[2] Schwartz, J., Van Berkel, A., Hodson, T., & Otten, I. W. (2014, March 07). The overwhelmed employee. http://bit.ly/HRtrends24

We live in a time where the only constant in business is change. It's a trite saying, but no less true. The technologies that were supposed to make life easier are instead making it complex. The speed of modern communication means that markets that used to be able to ignore news because it was already out of date by the time it became common knowledge, now react on a hair trigger to the slightest disturbance or anomaly. Businesses are constantly under pressure from countless invisible forces.

It's tempting to simply sit and wait for the storm to pass. The problem is, by the time it passes, a new storm has hit. So, things don't get better. Lost consumers don't come back. Prices don't recover. The pressure doesn't abate.

In the face of that maelstrom, it's all too easy for organizations and their employees to abandon the principles and standards that made them successful. It's easy to lose direction and become disconnected from who you are and what you stand for.

Worse, employees find themselves under increasing pressure to do "whatever it takes" to get results, in the process losing touch with their own principles and standards, and deepening their sense of overwhelm, stress and—ultimately—disconnection from the organization.

The only answer is a radical, deep-seated change to the culture of your organization and to how you lead.

Why "Rules of Engagement"?

Our litigious world relies on an abundance of rules and laws to determine right from wrong. It's as though society demands ever more regulation in the hope that it will help us navigate an increasingly complex and unpredictable world. It won't.

Meanwhile, the concept of engagement permeates the workplace more than ever before. Leaders are trying to figure out the magic formula to "engage" employees. The problem is, however, that engagement isn't something that can be "done" to people; it will happen naturally and spontaneously when individuals align purpose and feel valued.

So why did I use those two words—*rules* and *engagement*—in the title of my book? Because I believe we have looked at these words purely through the eyes of the organization for too long and now it's time to look at them through the eyes of the employee. The same words from a different perspective. It's a subtle distinction, but powerful.

In Part One of the book, I examine the changes to the business environment that make engagement so imperative. Then, in Part Two, I discuss how we need to adapt our notions of how we do business and how we manage our workplaces and workforces to reflect these new imperatives. Central to this is the creation of a new kind of culture: one that I call the Purposeful Workplace Experience™.

How do you build a Purposeful Workplace Experience? By following my four Rules of Engagement. That is the focus of Part Three, which describes the rules and how they can impact what gets done in the workplace. The rules of engagement will help you to build that new culture, and restore the lost connection and alignment. It is the "how" that you can combine with the "what"—the business strategy you already have in place—to decrease the overwhelm, increase engagement and, ultimately, drive direct bottom-line growth.

SHARE YOUR OWN STORY

I would love to hear your stories about using
the four rules of engagement to build
positive employee experiences in the workplace.

Use these hashtags:

#PWE

#PurposefulWorkplaceExperience

#RulesofEngagement

#WorkplaceCulture.

Don't forget to tag me in your posts!

Twitter - @PinnacleCarolyn

Instagram - @PinnacleWorkplaceCulture

LinkedIn – Carolyn Swora

PART ONE

Why Work Isn't Working

This section of the book explores how the world of work has changed, and why and how everyone needs to adapt: the individual, the team, the organization, and perhaps even society itself.

Chapter One

Running on Empty

People are exhausted and overwhelmed.
They are tired, sick and frustrated, and
work is taking all their energy.

Look beneath the surface of any modern office, and you'll realize that people are deluged with information throughout the day, too much of it. They spend their time trying to filter and manage the flood while also trying to meet the demands of their job. The inevitable result? They are overworked, overwhelmed and exhausted.

The *Global Human Capital Trends Report* first reported the issue of the "overwhelmed" employee in 2014. Since then, the problem has arguably only become worse, and the trend is spreading from overextended employees to overextended managers and leaders.

Overwhelm is the new normal, but how did we get to this point?

The First Curve

It starts with technology, what Bersin calls *the first curve*. The technology that was supposed to make working life easier is instead making it harder. And CEOs recognize the challenge: research by Deloitte suggests that 90% of CEOs believe their organization is facing disruptive change driven by digital technology.[3]

Technology makes information instantly accessible. The challenge is, that information often comes in its raw form. It is unedited, unclassified and—in that state—unusable. So, organizations are getting incrementally better at generating more data, but the technology isn't there to do the analysis and make the judgements that humans have to make on more and more data. At the same time, the messages our people get from the data are often contradictory, and so they need to dedicate time, energy and resources to making sense of those contradictions before they can even start to make decisions based on that information.

"Output" is not the same as "Productivity"

Next is the relentless pressure to win and be on top. That is often interpreted as a need to make better decisions faster—just as it's getting harder to do that. The dominant mindset, even among knowledge workers, is one of industrialized productivity, and many people simply equate "output" to success and energy (what I refer to as "industrial thinking").

And finally, that pressure has been intensified by the shortening of communication cycles. One hundred years ago, if you wanted to communicate with someone on the far side of the world, you wrote a letter, the letter was loaded on a

---

[3] Rewriting the rules for the digital age: *2017 Deloitte Global Human Capital Trends, page 30*

steamship, and if you were lucky, you got a reply three months later.

Ten years ago, you emailed someone or left a voicemail, and you hoped they would get back to you the next day.

Today, someone thousands of miles away can pick up a phone, send an email, a text or—more likely—an instant message, and get through to you instantly. And they expect an instant response.

All of these changes are compounding and coming together. Why are people exhausted and overwhelmed? Because they are not taking time to recover and slow down.

Look for the 'tells'

So, what does that stress and overwhelm look like in the workplace? How would a leader know that they or their employees are stressed and overwhelmed?

It shows up in many small but significant ways. You find yourself checking your phone every few seconds, even while you try to talk to others. In a meeting, people have their laptops open, and they're checking their email, instant messenger and social media feeds. They seem incapable of just shutting everything off and focusing. It is a very subtle, yet powerful indicator, and people often overlook it.

It shows up as an inability to find the information you are looking for or cite the source of something. You find yourself in meetings saying, "I know I have that somewhere, but I can't remember where. Let me get back to you."

When you add that to the constant flood of information, it becomes difficult to know what comes from a good source and what comes from a bad source; what is real data and what is made up; what's real news and what's fake news.

Overwhelm isn't incompetence

As a result of all of this, you may find yourself or your direct reports in a meeting saying things like "I'm not sure," "I haven't had time to get to that." "This is so complex, I don't have time to understand it." Or there may not be much discussion at all as people are afraid of added accountability.

The danger is, we'll interpret these as signs that someone isn't "up to the job." Along with the relentless pressure to succeed comes the expectation that you should be on top of all the information and inputs available to you, that you should understand all of it.

And so, in addition to overwhelm and exhaustion, our direct reports start to feel fear. That's a danger point for a leader: being surrounded by people who are afraid to admit that they don't know what they don't know. It becomes a vicious cycle. People stop appreciating how complex a situation really is.

When things are highly complex, you need diverse opinions; you need to deconstruct it into smaller pieces; and you need an openness to explore lines of thought that may or may not be the right ones. That takes time, and it takes a fear-free environment, both of which are lacking in many workplaces.

What shadow are you casting?

Are you surrounded by people who are exhausted and stressed? Are you feeling exhausted and stressed yourself?

Start by asking yourself how you feel about your situation, and how people around you perceive you.

Next, consider how your actions or words are contributing to the situation. If you are seeing stress or overwhelm in the people around you, how are you contributing to it?

> I used to work with a VP who absolutely loved her job and worked at it all hours. It was natural to her to respond to emails immediately and, because she was thinking about work all the time, she would send out emails at all hours of the night and day, even on weekends. What she didn't realize was the negative impact those emails were heaving on her team.
>
> When an email came in, people felt that they needed to open and respond to it right away. They worried that if they didn't respond immediately, the VP would assume they were slacking, or not committed to the organization.
>
> Even senior people on her team felt the pressure, let alone the more junior members.
>
> As soon as somebody spoke up, however, and pointed out the pressure they felt when an email came in late on a Saturday night, for example, she was horrified.
>
> A new team norm took shape that emails were not to be sent by anyone—even the VP—between 5pm on Fridays and 8am the following Monday.

The key thing to remember is that your intent may be great, but people don't see your intent: they only notice the impact you have on them. So you need to understand the impact that you are having on people around you.

Helen was an individual contributor who had been a manager in a previous role. She followed direction and got stuff done. Everybody valued that, and she was known for following through. She was also seen as a good, innovative thinker.

She wasn't a superstar, but she was a solid, constant performer who could be relied on. As a result, it was easy for people to keep giving her things to do.

Right now, in your organization, there's probably someone you can think of who is your 'Helen.' They have a smile on their face, they are always positive, and they're a great team player.

When I looked at Helen, though, I could see that the smile and the cheerful demeanour were a front. I stopped her in the hall one day and asked her how she was doing.

She said, "I'm fine. Why?" and I said, "you just don't seem yourself, so I just thought I'd ask."

A few days later I got an email. "Hey, would you have a few minutes for me?" I said, "Of course," and she booked a slot in my calendar.

When she came by, she broke down and cried in my office. When I asked her how she was, she wasn't feeling great at all, but she couldn't believe that I'd seen it. "I'm overwhelmed," she said. "I can't keep up with everything. My husband and kids are mad at me, I feel like my boss is mad at me, and I feel like I can't do anything

> right for anybody. I'm so tired, but I love what I do and don't want to let anybody down." She reminded me of myself in the weeks before I went on stress leave several years earlier, when I thought I was fine and I wasn't.
>
> I asked her if she had noticed a change in her ability to think and focus, and I suggested she consider going to see her doctor. She did, and she ended up taking two months' leave.

The interesting postscript to Helen's story is what happened next. Here was a solid performer that everyone relied on and valued. After her return from leave, however, people started to question her competence. But it wasn't just her current performance they questioned, they started to wonder whether they'd misjudged her; whether, perhaps, she hadn't been as good as they thought. After that, she was quickly sidelined.

It is astonishing that an organization would have a solid performer and not notice the transformation but rather write it off as that person "going off the boil." Sadly, however, it happens over and over again. Rather than question the system that is leading good people to be overwhelmed and burnt out, leaders would rather question the ability of the individual.

The Second Curve

The second curve expands on the concept of Exhaustion and Overwhelm. Individuals adapt to changes relatively quickly, but aren't pausing long enough to recover and assess the situation. Businesses take a little longer, and public policy eventually catches up when it can.

The pressures I just described will continue unless we do something to change the situation. And if we don't, that overwhelm our people are feeling will eventually stop us from moving any further forward.

Many managers and leaders argue that this is *the new normal*, and we should just get used to it. I agree: we do need to get used to it. The challenge is that we need to find new ways to deal with it, but many organizations simply try to adapt their old ways of doing things.

In the knowledge economy, the machinery that keeps your business going is the brain. But an overwhelmed brain runs much less efficiently—perhaps as low as 50% of its full potential. It's as though the machine had missing parts. A machine needs to be lubricated and maintained. It needs to be topped up. You can't run a car on empty and then complain when it stalls.

Sabre-tooth Tigers in Suits

We have reached, and passed, a tipping point. Many of our best workers are chronically underproductive. To understand why, we need to examine how the human brain—that wonderful machine that drives our business—developed.

If you were to split a brain down the centre, you would see three layers, each of which developed at different stages of our evolution and fulfils a different purpose (Figure 1).

Closest to the surface, and last to evolve, is the *Neo-Cortex*, which is responsible for logic, rational thinking, consciousness, and imagination.

A little deeper, we come to the *Mammalian Brain*. This is the seat of emotions, responsible for processing feelings.

Finally, deep in the centre of the brain, sitting atop the spinal column, is a small area called the *Reptile Brain*. This is the oldest part of the brain and basiclly controls our survival responses.

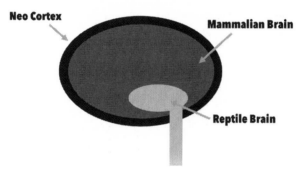

Figure 1: The Three Parts of the Brain

The Reptile Brain evolved with one main function: to keep you alive, which it does by monitoring for danger and responding in one of three basic ways: *fight, flight* or *fright*. In other words, faced with danger, our body responds by either making a stand, running away, or freezing (playing dead).

Here's where things get interesting. Remember where the Reptile Brain is: at the top of the spinal column. In other words, when a nerve impulse comes into the brain, the first part of the brain that gets to evaluate it is the Reptile Brain. You don't get to respond to danger logically, or even emotionally, until your Reptile Brain is sure the danger has passed.

I remember once driving along a country road. There was a truck in front of me that I wanted to pass. It was a quiet road, so even though I couldn't see past the truck, I accelerated and pulled out only to realize there was another car coming at me head-on, at full speed. Without thinking, I swerved back onto my side of the road (flight), misjudged slightly, and bumped along on the grass beside the highway as I stood on the brakes. I sat for a moment, unable to move or even think (fright) as my hands clenched the wheel, and then, after what seemed a lifetime, it slowly dawned on me how close I had come to not making it, and I broke down (the emotional response). My Mammalian Brain didn't get to 'do its thing' until my Reptile Brain was sure the danger had passed.

In other words, you can't engage your higher functions while your Reptile Brain perceives that you're in danger. It's a phenomenon I once heard summed up perfectly as "you can't write a symphony when you're drowning."

And our people are drowning. They're drowning in data. They're weighed down by deadlines. They're suffocated by a corporate culture that says it's not OK to say you're not OK. And yet, we still demand they create symphonies for us.

Those survival mechanisms evolved to keep us safe from predators. For a caveman facing a sabre-toothed tiger, a sudden boost of adrenaline to get him running or give him extra strength to fight was exactly what was needed. The problem is, the Reptile Brain responds to modern threats exactly the same way it responded to those earlier threats. It can't tell the difference between a looming deadline and a pouncing tiger, and so it gives us that same adrenaline rush that says 'get ready to respond to danger.' But we can't. When someone tells you they need a report a day earlier, you can't stab them with a spear. When your boss corners you in a meeting and demands information you don't have available, you can't run away. When you miss the monthly reporting deadline, you can't curl up in the corner of the office and play dead.

What's that got to do with my team?

Business has developed to prize the logical functions of the Neo-Cortex above all else. It's an appealing model. To the logical brain, the world is a black and white place. Answers are either right or wrong. We do, or we don't. It makes decisions simple, and it makes decisions easy to explain: we just need to back them up with logic and data.

So, you've got an environment that praises and supports only the rational, logical part of the brain, and a group of people who are primed to respond primitively to threats. We have forgotten about the emotional brain in the middle.

We've lost connection, and we need to restore it, which is why—as you'll see later in the book—the first rule of the Purposeful Workplace Experience™ is *connect with people not process.*

As leaders and managers, we need to connect to people in our organization and listen to those emotional signals—our own and those of our people. People are the critical element in keeping the modern corporate machine running.

The Vicious Cycle

As we get busier and more overwhelmed, we stop thinking and fall into a vicious cycle that overvalues extraversion and status.

Increasing prosperity and increasing responsibility created a culture where people feel the need to brag about how busy they are, and for a while, it really became a status symbol: "I'm really busy. We just closed a major deal, and we stayed up all night."

The system rewarded you for it, and that, in turn, gave you something else to brag about. And that was fine, while people remained productive. But the world has changed, and the culture hasn't caught up: we still assume that if someone is busy, they must be productive.

As Susan Cain points out in her book *Quiet*, our society places an inordinate amount of value on the extroverted personality. For many years, we listened to the loudest voice in the room, and that voice was bragging about how much money they made, or the deal they closed.

Rather than fight the overwhelm, it's easier for an employee to simply disconnect, emotionally and psychologically, from their job and from the company. That's ironic when you consider that it was the fear of disconnection that made them say nothing in the first place.

So, now, they're not operating from a place of authenticity. They're not thinking about what they do. All that matters is getting through the day, and it's easier to mimic what they think the company wants. They are trying to live up to, and be like, everybody else.

They just follow the crowd, which means that now they have to disconnect from themselves: from their own values. They are choosing to connect with others and be part of the herd, at the cost of sacrificing themselves.

So, imagine yourself as one of those disconnected employees—and it could just as easily be a manager or an executive. Each day, you come to work, you keep your head down, and you make decisions that may or may not be in line with your own values and your sense of self. What's worse, you stop caring: you accept that it's the price you have to pay to fit in. And you think you can live with yourself until one day when something happens, and you suddenly think *"Holy ****, what have I been doing?"* In my own case, that day came when Paul was diagnosed in March 2003. It was a life-changing event, and it forced me to re-evaluate my priorities. I suddenly realized that I didn't have to follow everyone else.

The first time I disconnected was when Paul got sick. At the time, I was six-months pregnant. It wasn't that I hated my company. It was simply a dawning realization that *"this can't be the centre of my world anymore. I have to look at my priorities differently."*

I was well known within the company, and because of everything I was going through, people didn't judge me for my ups and downs. It was like having the 'Get out of jail free" card in Monopoly. It didn't give me permission to do whatever I wanted or treat people badly. It just meant that I could let go of worrying about what other people were thinking, because I had other priorities at home.

That was my first disconnection—it wasn't a bad disconnection, more a reprioritization and taking back control. That was important, because you need to have that reset, and understand what you are connected to.

I loved working at the company. It was an environment I thrived in. We had a great corporate culture, we met our business objectives, we had amazing training and development opportunities.

As happens in every industry, we hit a point where our numbers started to go down and in order to meet budget we had to decrease headcount. With that came the change initiatives. You were expected to do more with fewer people, and everybody was trying to keep up with the new way of working and the new expectations.

Around the time that Paul passed away was when it all started to accelerate. At the same time, my perception of what was going on changed. I had dealt with Paul's illness, and I wasn't in a daze anymore. All I could see was people getting increasingly disconnected. At every level of the organization, they were caught up in the process and struggling to keep up. I saw it happening at the higher levels first, even though they all thought they were fine. The more that it happened, the more I disconnected.

Now, you might be reading this and thinking, *"But your case is special. No one on my team has a dying spouse. They don't have these pressures going on at home, so why do I need to pay attention to this?"* Well, it's not just about life-changing events. People will disconnect, and they won't need a major family event or a crisis for it to happen. And the way we do business is a major factor.

Here is an example from a former colleague in their own words.

"The signs were there if anyone had cared to notice. As I disconnected from my employer, my manager, and my team, I became cynical.

"I would see key messages coming down from Corporate Communications that I was supposed to communicate to my team and be a champion for. Instead, I would think *'OK, this is the same **** over and over again. Can we not be a little more authentic?'*

"I knew it was a stage everybody goes through in their corporate career, but I wanted to cut to the chase and have an honest conversation. I was sick of the prefabricated messages.

"I also realized that I didn't enjoy going into work in the way I had. That was a real reversal for me: I loved the company, even when I was tasked with something I didn't enjoy doing, because any experience is an opportunity to learn. But I started getting cynical, bored and unfocused, and it became a real effort to go to work.

"Before the change, I was a high flyer; a model employee and manager. Now, here I was, every leader's worst nightmare: as a manager, I was the one the company relied on to rally everyone around new initiatives, but I was the one who was cynical."

It's interesting at this point to note that you won't always see the change. In this case, they kept the cynicism to themselves. They didn't openly challenge the messages they were asked to convey; they just didn't embrace them.

Somewhere in your team, right now, there's probably a manager who is torn and conflicted. They know what you expect from them, but they just can't find it in themselves to deliver it. They do the job, but they don't put everything they could into it. Not because they're an underperformer, but because they've disconnected from the job, from you, and from the message.

In my own case, I continued to toe the company line. I knew how important it was for me, as a manager, to be seen to support the messages. I also recognized that, ultimately, a manager is just a number; they're not bigger than the company (That's a big statement to make, and in Chapter Four, I'll explore that theme in detail).

But I too became disconnected. The company and I were falling out of love. Sometimes, in a relationship, you can find your way back from that, but I realized that, whether we could find our way back or not, it was not something I wanted to do. I just wanted to break up and go away.

I was never a thorn in my manager's side. I got stuff done. The problem for my manager was that, in less than a year, I went from being a top performer to being a performance issue. They made it my problem, as performance management processes always do, but looking back, it wasn't *my* problem, it was all of ours.

The danger is, if you have a real high-flyer, you may not initially spot the change because their *B-game* still looks better than a lot of other people's *A-game*.

Worse still, if you have a manager who has been a top performer, and suddenly they start to underperform, you may not always look for the problem in the right place. It's tempting to look at a manager who is suddenly dipping and think "perhaps she doesn't have the right people on her team."

How this Impacts the Customer

Every business has a customer they are selling to, and most companies deliver a mediocre customer experience at best. Customers have to make do with, "Hi, can I help you?" rather than "Oh my gosh! Thanks for visiting our store!" (or calling our hotline, or ordering our product, or whatever interaction customers have with you). Many employees just don't go out of their way to make a different experience for somebody, which is not hard to understand in light of what I wrote above.

At the same time, productivity has declined. It can seem like we're more productive, but that is simply because there is more work to be done. But people are unfocused and overwhelmed, and that impacts not just productivity but creativity and critical thinking. That's devastating for performance and for decision-making, but it's hard to judge the cost of deciding on one course of action over another. It's hard to put a cost on lost creativity or ideas that weren't generated. You can't put a value on innovation that didn't happen.

They're all lost opportunities. And companies tend to think about it more often in the context of systems and processes, but employees have to make decisions, they need to innovate, they need to be able to evaluate a situation critically: that's how we deliver exceptional products, services or experiences to customers.

But instead of addressing the real issue that's keeping service mediocre, the easy path is just to send people off for more training, or time management, or provide coaching so they can progress their career more quickly.

As we'll see when we look at the hierarchy of human needs, however, people aren't going to respond to the coaching and training, etc., as long as the problems—and the feeling of overwhelm—are still there. As long as they feel disconnected from their values and their purpose. As long as they feel threatened psychologically and emotionally.

That's why the Purposeful Workplace Experience™, which I introduce later in this book, isn't about coaching and training. It's about creating an environment for people to think and connect.

Summary

- ❖ Technology makes information instantly accessible but current technology doesn't allow us to analyze it as fast as it's coming in.
- ❖ This is contributing to employees working in a state of constant overwhelm and exhaustion.
- ❖ The brain has three major components:
  - o Reptile brain – fight, flight or fright response
  - o Mammalian brain – emotions and feelings
  - o Neo-cortex – logic and rational thinking
- ❖ "Overwhelmed" does not equal "incompetent" but it is leading many to live in a constant state of fight, flight or fright.
- ❖ Our workplace values logic and rational thinking. The emotional part of brain is being overlooked and undervalued.
- ❖ As a result, many people are disconnecting from work.

Chapter Two

Why Leaders Need to Pay Attention

There used to be an element of stability and predictability in our working world that systems and processes relied upon. Not anymore. A new approach is needed if you want your business to survive.

Ultimately, this book is not about people, it's about making money by focusing on people. It's about grabbing lost opportunities for profit and growth. It's about the ability to respond quickly in a marketplace that is changing rapidly and often unpredictably. It's about reducing employee turnover, so you don't have to spend time and money training and retraining and making up for lost continuity.

Each time a team changes, it loses productivity. Each time someone leaves or joins, the whole team has to go back and reform. It disrupts the relationships already in place. It's not just about one individual having to come up to speed; it's the team having to recover.

Since 2013, leadership research by both Gallup and Bersin by Deloitte has found that senior management and CEOs are recognizing the importance of employee engagement and culture, that it does impact profitability.

The problem is, senior leaders don't know what to do, they don't know where to start, but they feel that they should be able to figure things out. They get trapped in a worldview that says that no outsider is going to know their business better than they do, that their business is different from any other business, and therefore they don't need to reach outside for help. And even if they do have an open mind, the chances are they're too busy to recognize the problem in the first place.

That is why it is hard to break out: because leaders don't recognize that experts can come in and help.

Part of that transformation is to help the internal HR function and leaders to transition into the role of human performance consultants: they aren't there to manage, direct and control; they are there to help elevate performance, and help managers become leaders in their own right.

If the organization is to keep up with the technology and the processes, they are going to have to bring in external experts to help with the human performance side of things, and allow HR to do more than simply managing processes.

The old ways don't work anymore

The 80s and 90s were a time of predictability and control. Managing an organization was very much like managing the efficiencies of a machine. Things were very stable, so that approach worked well.

We didn't have the technology at our disposal that we do now: back then telephones were still anchored to the wall by a cable!

That lack of technology, especially communication technology, meant you were forced to connect with people and have conversations—and there was time available to do this.

That personal communication and connection built and strengthened relationships, which are the glue that binds organizations together. On a logical level, it was an inefficient way of communicating, but it was very efficient from the point of view of collaboration: it was about control, efficiency, and predictability.

Innovation didn't happen at the speed it does today. People worked in silos; you were rewarded for working in your silo, and individual performance was highly admired, as was bragging and posturing about individual performance! It was seen as a weakness if you had to ask other people for help or support.

The other characteristic of those times, from an organizational perspective, was a lack of checks and balances. Sarbanes Oxley was still in the future. Enron hadn't happened yet. Accountability was deferred, and secrecy was admired and respected.

The other thing missing was diversity of *thought*. Information was held on a need-to-know basis and guarded jealously by people in positions of power, so it was easier to pull the wool over people's eyes: no-one was going to trawl through the microfiches in the corporate library to fact check you.

Welcome to the new millennium

That command and control approach no longer works, and it no longer serves us. You can't drive employee efficiency through fear and control. You can't simply manage from the top down.

How you work matters, and employees need to know what the leaders are doing. And those leaders need to be authentic: integrity in <u>how</u> you work is just as important as what you do.

Of course, right now, as I write this, I'm talking about white collar jobs, knowledge workers; in an industrial setting, the old ways of command and control can still apply. For now.

Summary

* ❖ CEOs acknowledge that employee engagement impacts profitability.
* ❖ Predictability, control and secrecy defined organizations in the past, but this mindset no longer drives employee efficiency.
* ❖ "How" you work is now just as important as the results you can deliver.

Chapter Three

Look Outside the Company

The workplace is being disrupted by major
forces outside of your organization.
Understanding those forces is critical to your
success.

So, what is happening in the outside world?

There are four major forces at play that are shaping how we
live and how we work:

- Globalization

- Disintermediation

- Technology

- Demographics

Globalization

It's not that long ago that even global companies were able
to operate each national subsidiary as a separate entity. There
might be a global strategy driving big picture objectives, but
overall, country managers were free to set their own agenda
and to respond to their local markets as they saw fit.

Those days are gone. Increasingly, global companies operate on a global scale. Supply chains now span continents. Teams can include people in every corner of the planet. And managers have to respond to changes, not only in their own markets but in markets halfway around the world.

You can't plan that response in a bubble. Because of globalization, you need a broader perspective of the organization and its industry. Fortunately, we now have faster and better access to information than at any time in history. Twenty years ago, it would have been very hard to see emerging trends and what is going on in the world. Today, it doesn't take much digging.

Of course, knowledge workers tend to be more mobile and more willing to go somewhere else. The ability to work globally is no longer reserved for the elite. The opportunity is offered to people much earlier, but that just means that many global corporations no longer feel the need to open a local head office in every country where they operate. Instead, they run local operations as remote operations, and top talent is shipped back to the 'homeland'.

Disintermediation

The next major trend is disintermediation: the drive to cut the middleman out of transactions.

In the *old economy*, consumers were dependent on an intermediary—a salesperson, an agent, a distributor or whoever—for the information they needed.

Today, you can invest your own stocks, buy your own car, book your own travel. Disintermediation redefines the relationship between the user and the product. It has even happened in health care. When medical information first started to appear on the internet, doctors were horrified—and offended—if a patient dared to turn up for an appointment with a self-diagnosis. How *dare* the patient look up their symptoms on the web! What medical school had Google attended? Now, it is normal for a patient to arrive, diagnosis in hand, and say "OK doctor, I have XYZ, tell me my treatment." Or, you may go even further. Perhaps you've heard about a drug trial that's taking place, and you ask to be put on it.

The biggest shifts have been in the retail sector. The internet gives you direct access to manufacturers and suppliers, and makes the entire world your showroom. And there's no salesperson sharing features, prices or benefits.

That spills over into the labour market. You no longer have the polished, experienced customer service agents that you used to get in retail. It's now an entry-level job and, inevitably, you don't get the good customer service that you used to.

It's a ticking time bomb in our workforce. While globalization has destroyed many blue-collar jobs, disintermediation is eliminating many white-collar jobs.

Technology

The fundamental shift that powers globalization and disintermediation is technology.

Technology enables real-time communication over long distances. It gives us immediate access to information. That, in turn, has increased the cost of entry for companies. When you launch a business, having a storefront is no longer enough: you have to have an online presence, including mobile (because people are going to be buying on their phone).

If your business deals in physical products, then the chances are that a lot of your supply chain is going to be global; you'll be sourcing parts from China and elsewhere.

If you're selling to other businesses, they are going to expect your systems to tie into their systems as well. If you're part of their supply chain, you have to be able to deliver a purchase order or shipping notification electronically in the format they expect.

Behind the scenes, processes have also been globalized and disintermediated by technology. Employees access all the information they need through self-service portals. On the one hand, they feel empowered: *Hey, I have access to all these tools now, that's great!* On the other hand, it is also a fundamental point in our disconnection, as now we have all this information, but we have to find it ourselves.

All this information is wonderful, but it is unfiltered, and no one has the time to critically evaluate it.

So, it's great that an employee can go online and, in five minutes, they have found an answer. But in six minutes, they can find five hundred answers, and now they have to decide which is the *right* answer.

The recent rise of cloud computing allows small and medium-sized businesses to access corporate-level data centres and compete directly with major companies. Industries that were once protected by the need for a massive investment in technology anymore are no longer protected. You don't need to build a data centre yourself anymore; Amazon will do it for you.

Enter the Millennials

The 2016 Global Human Capital Trends report highlights an interesting demographic shift in the workplace. For the first time ever, we have six decades represented in the workforce. As a result, employers have to meet a wide range of often conflicting needs.

It's almost expected now for business books to talk about millennials, as though they are somehow a different species that managers have to study and learn to co-exist with. I am not going to single out millennials as though they were the only generation with needs: all generations have them.

Where millennials *are* different is that they are much better than earlier generations at articulating those needs, and walking away from a job if they don't get those needs met— something that we will return to later in the book when we discuss the Psychological Contract.

So, what has this done to companies?

At the top, you have a senior layer, who grew up in a very different time. They have a very different set of expectations compared to this newest generation, which creates a real gap in understanding. They look at millennials, coming into the workforce and making 'demands', and they wonder how these young upstarts can be so entitled. Millennials, for their part, feel that the older generation doesn't listen to them and doesn't value them because of a perceived lack of experience—work experience and life experience. That only serves to expand the generation gap.

Then we add another layer to that generation gap. Because millennials have been more vocal in expressing their needs, and their disappointment if those needs aren't met, they've received a lot of attention. Suddenly, you can't go into a bookstore without finding half a dozen books about how to handle millennials. Business journals are full of articles about the challenge of dealing with millennials. It can feel, at times, as though no other generation gets as much attention paid to them.

Leaders need to acknowledge that every generation is important. Every generation contributes to the success of the organization. Every generation is simply a collection of individuals. Those individuals have their own needs, but—as we will see in Chapter 6—there are common, basic needs shared by everyone.

Ultimately, people drive the success of the organization, but looking for different ways to drive the success of people is not the answer. The core of the Purposeful Workplace Experience™ is that organizations don't need to have completely different approaches, tailored to every employee. They simply need to focus on meeting the core needs and creating an environment in which individuals can be allowed to meet their other needs.

People hate to change

One of the things we strive for is stability and predictability. Change—particularly the sweeping, all-encompassing change that is now a constant feature of business life—challenges that need.

This is not a book on brain science, so I won't go into the mechanics but, hopefully, you recognize that when things are stable, we feel safer; we know what's going to happen; we can plan a response. We feel like we have control—it's actually only the illusion of control because, in reality, we don't—but when you don't know what's coming, it's hard to prepare. That's what causes stress and anxiety for people.

Now, stress isn't always a bad thing—there is such a thing as 'good' stress, which can help us improve our performance—but in some situations, that stress can get out of control. It happens when you don't know how far the situation is going to go. It happens when you are operating in a culture or environment of fear—say, an environment in which you're afraid to make mistakes, or that you'll be perceived as slacking or uncommitted. And, of course, some people are just more anxious than others. If any of those situations hold true, it basically means you are in this constant state of stress, with no time to slow down or recover. And when that's true, unpredictability just becomes even scarier.

So, the reality is it's not that people don't like change *per se*. What they object to is the stress of not knowing what is going to happen. In that heightened state, as we saw, your reptile brain goes into *fight, flight* or *fright*—and whether you fight the change, threaten to resign, or simply do nothing when you're asked to change, it's going to be interpreted as resistance.

2016—the year the world went mad

That resistance doesn't just show up in the workplace. If 2016 showed the world one thing, it is that people hate change. The two political seismic shifts of that year—Brexit in the UK and the election of Donald Trump as 45th president of the United States—were a very public rejection of the forces of globalization and disintermediation that I mentioned above. Ultimately, of course, those movements play well to supporters, but they are doomed to fail. No one person or people—or even one country for that matter—is going to be able to stop this.

We need to have checks and balances, and from that point of view—regardless of how you feel about Trump and Brexit—they are both valuable checkpoints. They have forced the world to stop and think about what is happening. In the long term, those events will have aligned people more strongly, however divisive they have been in the short term.

Of course, CEOs, leaders, and managers aren't immune to that mindset.

They have the same need for stability. They have the same desire to keep their stress at a level they can cope with. They need to feel back in control.

It's about more than 'Change Management'

So, how do companies—and leaders—need to change to adapt to this harsh new world?

It starts with a concept called "VUCA": Volatility, Uncertainty, Complexity, and Ambiguity

These four letters impact our day, every day, and we don't even know it. They define the world within which we operate. They also make change inevitable.

The VUCA model has its origins in the US military academy. In war, the enemy hardly ever does what you want them to. They stubbornly refuse to follow your battle plan. In other words, you just don't know what they're going to do, so you have to plan for different options.

So, companies need to embrace the concept of VUCA, and help employees to let go of the expectation of predictability and stability; to understand that is not the world we live in.

Next, you need to help your people to understand that technology is constantly changing. Now, most people can connect with that, because they see it happening around them, but it's one of those things they can't predict.

This chaos and unpredictability feed into how companies plan. They are planning differently and acknowledging the chaos. Risk mitigation plans are more rigorous than they ever used to be. They are no longer seen as a box-checking exercise; instead, emergency planning and disaster recovery are standard in all industries. Scenario planning—preparing variations of the plan to allow for different external factors— has also become more popular.

Leaders need to be comfortable in this new world. The May-June 2017 issue of Harvard Business Review[4] highlighted the findings of a ten-year study by ghSmart's CEO Genome

---

[4] *Lytkina Botelho, E., Rosenkoetter Power, K., Kincaid, S., & Wang, D. (2017, May & June). What sets successful CEOs apart. Harvard Business Review.*

Project, which concluded that "successful chief executives tend to demonstrate four specific behaviours that prove critical to their performance." That list of behaviours included "the ability to proactively adjust to a rapidly changing environment."

The Forces That Shape the World

Let's look at each element of VUCA in turn.

Volatility

V stands for *volatility*. This is the opposite of *stability*.

It is a word we often associate with stock markets, where it refers to a high degree of variation. We hear it used to describe the behaviour of a person or a mob, where it suggests violence is about to break out. And finally, we hear it, more and more often, attached to prices as the cost of goods and services rises and falls suddenly and unpredictably in response to some item of news.

In business, volatility often takes the form of changes in trends and consumer preferences. It is the opposite of being stable, so you can't predict anything anymore, and it's really about the speed and turbulence of change.

In part, it relates back to something I discussed earlier in this chapter. I said that companies now have immediate access to information and that, as a result, it's much harder to analyze that information and make informed decisions.

That also applies to consumers. They, too, have access to a lot more information. They, too, struggle to make sense of it. As a result, they react to events as they happen. A piece of news comes up, and a customer decides to cancel their order. A week later, the news has changed, and they are back on the phone ordering more again.

Uncertainty

U stands for *uncertainty*, the opposite of predictability. It means that you don't know what is going to happen. And when you don't know what is going to happen, it is hard to plan and predict.

How do these two forces interact? Think of a wave machine in a swimming pool: the peaks and troughs come at predictable intervals, and they are all the same height and depth.

If we introduce *volatility*, those peaks become higher and the troughs become deeper. But also, each peak is not necessarily the same height as the one before or the one after, and the depths will vary too. The one thing that does not change is the rhythm: the peaks and troughs continue to come at predictable intervals.

If we now add *uncertainty*, the rhythm changes. The gap between peaks and troughs changes, so that you no longer know when the wave is going to hit you.

In other words, uncertainty means you know there are going to be highs and lows, but you don't know when. Volatility means you don't know how big those highs and lows will be.

Uncertainty can also happen when you don't have all the information available to you, or—in this over-informed world we have created—when you don't know whether you have the *right* information in the mountain of data you've collected.

Complexity

C stands for *complexity*. Globalization and technology have played a major role in making the world a more complex place.

When you are doing business across borders, you have different regulations to deal with. The more borders you cross, the more regulations you have to contend with, and the more opportunities there are for those regulations to conflict with each other.

When you are doing business with other businesses, you have to deal with different systems. As technology increases, the complexity in how these different systems and tools speak to each other increases. And the more organizations you have in your supply chain, the harder it becomes to get all those systems to communicate and the more opportunities there are for something to go wrong.

Managers need to learn to stop thinking linearly. We need to deconstruct each situation; to break it down and understand the different variables; to understand and simplify. That is a skill that is not taught well to managers. Business education focuses on "if X happens, do Y."

Think of launching a new product. In the modern business environment, we may have a global supply chain for manufacturing that product. So, we have to consider how to get parts from one continent to another. We have to deal with customs regulations, insurance, logistics. We have to coordinate production, purchasing, and deliveries: it's expensive to have a warehouse full of component A, which came from a company 100 miles away, while we wait six months for component B to be manufactured and shipped from China or Australia. There's an increasingly complex web of stakeholders to consider in the launch: customers, stakeholders, employees, vendors, regulators, governments, communities, and more. Each of those groups has different requirements, and managing those requirements is complex and time-consuming.

Ambiguity

A stands for *ambiguity*. This refers to the fact that you have to make decisions when you don't have a simple 'yes' or 'no' answer. That's difficult, because other people often demand clear-cut answers: "yes or no?" "A or B?" "Go or no-go?" They don't want to hear "Maybe" or "Unless…" or "What if?"

Faced with those demands, leaders will sometimes give in to pressure and default into giving a 'yes' or 'no' answer and then have to backtrack. If you had the time, you could go and get the extra information you need to reduce the ambiguity, but you don't have the time, and the world may change while you're still gathering information, so you have to learn to make decisions without necessarily clear solutions. Worse still, you may gather the information you need and find that the situation is so complex, so unpredictable, so volatile, that the data simply increases the ambiguity of the situation.

Of course, as a leader, the chances are you expect similarly clear-cut answers from those who report to you.

You have to recognize—and allow your employees to recognize—that it's no longer simply a matter of wrong or right; it's about what makes sense with the information we have available right now, knowing that tomorrow it could change. It's about allowing people to make a decision that is correct today, knowing that they won't be chastised if the situation reverses overnight and makes the decision wrong.

How VUCA Helps Us Change

Now, it's all well and good understanding that there is volatility, uncertainty, complexity, and ambiguity in the world, but how does that help me to be a better leader?

You have to understand your operating environment. You have to understand the forces that are at work in your world. That may sound basic, but it is powerful.

Now, VUCA isn't an analytical model. You *could* sit down during a planning session and ask, "Here is our objective. How volatile are the circumstances around our ability to meet it? What kind of unpredictability have we seen here before?" and so on, but that's not where its power is.

The key point to VUCA is that it's a reminder. It's a reminder of why the world is so chaotic and crazy, and why it isn't going to get any better. And it's a reminder that however "well" we plan, the market is going to throw something unexpected at us and we need to be ready to respond.

That, in turn, means that we need to stop being controlled by industrial thinking. Industrial thinking doesn't fit in a VUCA world. Our systems, behaviours, and processes were set up in a different era: one of predictability and stability. We are like infants banging a round peg into a square hole, and we just keep pounding as if it's actually going to fit one day. We may not be having a tantrum on the outside like a toddler would, but inside we are screaming.

It also requires a new mindset of leadership. It's no longer about figuring out what to do, and then telling people and measuring it. We have to take a new approach to how organizations operate by recognizing that relationships are at the heart of business success and finding ways to nurture relationships efficiently and authentically. That's the only way you are going to manage the VUCA.

Summary

❖ Four major forces are disrupting our workplace and how we operate: globalization, disintermediation, technology and demographics.

❖ VUCA defines our working environment
  o Volatility – the opposite of stability
  o Uncertainty – the opposite of predictability
  o Complexity – lots of stakeholders, integration of systems and conflicting regulations
  o Ambiguity – answers aren't always straightforward

Chapter Four

New Workplace, New Rules

Between every employee and their
employer, there is a contract of employment
that neither side ever signed. It is
unenforceable in a court of law, and yet it
governs the daily interactions that happen
in offices, stores and factories the world over.
When an employer lets go of someone, it is
sometimes because they breached the
formal written contract of employment.
When someone quits, it is almost always
because their manager or the company
breached the *unwritten* contract.

The Psychological Contract

We call this unwritten contract—which is made up primarily
of all the mutual beliefs, perceptions and informal expectations that arise over the course of someone's employment—
the Psychological Contract.

The terms of the psychological contract encompass the expectations an employee—or the workforce in general—have
towards the employer; things like the rights, obligations, and
rewards the employee believes they are entitled to in return
for their work and loyalty.

Depending on what is already covered by the formal contract
of employment, the psychological contract might include

- How flexible the work environment is: work from home policies, maternity leave, parental leave, 'personal time' (for medical appointments, school meetings, etc.), being able to take time off if you work through the night.

- How efforts or ideas are respected or heard or appreciated in meetings.

- Mobility and what opportunities will be offered.

- Supervision (e.g., whether—or how much—they will be micromanaged), what level freedom they think they have, the discretion to make decisions, how much trust they will be given.

- Flexibility, in terms of spending budget.

- How much 'fun' they can expect to have in the workplace: is the workplace all fun or all serious? Can you laugh at a meeting?

How does this contract arise? Some of it is set by the market: we see how employees in other organizations are treated, and we expect to be treated similarly. In that sense, the market can change how we feel about our employer and the terms of our employment, even if nothing changes on paper. That introduces VUCA into the employment relationship, because VUCA can change the market, which in turn impacts how the psychological contract evolves. But how do you track something that is informal, unwritten and—for the most part-unconscious?

The other way it arises is through the day-to-day interactions between the company, the leaders and managers, and the employees. Implicit in that is the expectation that if the manager or company treats one person or team one way, they are going to be that way with everybody. Everything you do as a leader—how you interact with one employee or another, what you do yourself in the course of your day, how you allocate responsibility—can (and frequently does) become part of the psychological contract.

That is a major challenge, because much of the contract is about perception, and everybody's perception is different. Perceptions can change over time, and they are never formalized, so it is easy to dismiss them because we can't track them or measure them. That doesn't make them any less critical.

Now, because it arises from employees' observations of how things get done in the workplace, the psychological contract is a collective arrangement. You don't have a psychological contract with every employee individually—if you did, it means you'd be playing favourites, treating some employees better than others. Instead, the psychological contract exists between the company and its workforce.

Two Icebergs Colliding

Icebergs are popular in business books. They're a great way to show that there are some things that you can observe and measure—just like the parts of an iceberg above the water— but there is a lot more going on under the surface that you can't see.

So, yes, I'm going to use icebergs as a metaphor, but just for a moment.

You can think of both sides of the psychological contract—the employees and the organization—as icebergs: as I said, there are things going on above the surface that we can observe, and a lot more happening below the surface, which we can't see.

When we consider the employee, we can observe their skills, their actions and behaviours, and the results those actions and behaviours generate. That is what is above the waterline.

Beneath the waterline, if we could look, we would discover their beliefs and values, their sense of self—who they believe themselves to be—and their motivations.

Similarly, when we consider the organization, we see the actions it takes in the world and the results those actions have. That includes both what it does in the "outside world"—how it does business and how (and what) it communicates—and what it does in the "inside world"—how it interacts with its employees. We can also observe its documented processes, and the metrics the company chooses to track. All of that is above the waterline. Below the waterline, and hidden from view, you find the organizational values and beliefs that drive its actions, its corporate identity, and its motivations.

Figure 2: The Employee and the Company as Icebergs

USE IN poster

In many ways, then, the psychological contract arises as each side observes the other and tries to guess what is below the surface, based—as I said earlier—on perception.

That means that the higher that water level is—the more we feel is being hidden by either side—the less trust there will be between the parties. By the same token, the more each side can lower the water level—by revealing more of what is below the surface—the more trust there will be.

The Balance of Power

The psychological contract is not a new concept. It was first described in 1960 by Chris Argyris of Harvard Business School and further developed in a 1989 article by Denise Rousseau[5].

What has changed in that time is the balance of power in the relationship. Until recently, employers held much of the power: the organization set the rules, and you either agreed or not. If they changed the rules, you—as an employee—had to decide whether to stay or go, and normally people chose to stay. A big part of the psychological contract was about tenure and job security: if you did what you were asked to do, you could work there for as long as you wanted to. It was not unusual to find employees who had been with the same company for decades; in some cases, for their entire career.

In recent years, of course, job security has been eroded, and the idea of a job for life has disappeared altogether. That was

---

[5] Rousseau, D. M. (1989). Psychological and implied contracts in organizations. Employee Responsibilities and Rights Journal , 2: 121-139.

much easier to promise when markets were stable. As a result, employees are far more willing to walk away if they don't like the terms of the psychological contract. In a world where each employee is just a row on a spreadsheet, each employer becomes just a paragraph on a resume.

The role of trade unions used to be to ensure that the psychological contract could be backed by a written contract, without leaving a lot of space for interpretation. A common cry was "a fair day's work for a fair day's pay."

In the new normal, however, what is "a fair day's work?" When does a fair day's work finish: 5pm, 8pm, when the work is done? And what is "fair pay" for a role?

VUCA has destabilized the psychological contract and pushed more of the iceberg below the surface, making it even harder to track and measure.

The culmination of these shifts is increased use of fixed-term contractors—even in white collar jobs—the move towards the gig economy (in which employees aren't even legally considered an employee), and zero-hour casual contracts (where the employer provides no guaranteed minimum hours). These represent the total breakdown of the psychological contract by setting out that there are to be *no* expectations on either side beyond what is on paper.

Managers and the Psychological Contract

Olivia was a colleague of mine who neatly illustrates how the psychological contract got broken. She was two levels below her VP. In every interaction the VP had with her, he was pompous and arrogant. She didn't feel heard, listened to, or respected. Instead, she was patronized and ignored. Her VP's attitude was that she should feel honoured and lucky to be in the role she was in.

One day, without warning, she simply said, "I'm done. I quit. I'm out." She walked back to her office, handed in her computer, walked out and never came back.

It had been building over time, but no-one saw it coming. Even afterward, people thought she would come back the following day to discuss what was going on.

This was someone who was married with two children. She wasn't a rebel or a risk taker. When she walked out, she didn't even have a plan. She'd simply had enough of having the psychological contract completely ignored.

Managers are often stuck in the middle, between leaders and front-line employees. That's a frustrating position to be in. On one side, you have your team members, airing their needs, their demands, and their frustrations. On the other side, they have senior leaders or the HR team complaining about the increasing demands and expectations of the workforce—leaders increasingly use the term "entitled" disparagingly when they talk about their team.

The manager is sitting between the two sides, and feeling pressure from both of them. When you add the fact that management isn't just about managing, dealing with, and leading people—there's usually an operational role as well—it's adding to the overwhelm that the manager is already experiencing.

Bear in mind that a lot of those demands from employees are things that wouldn't have had to be expressed before—they were part of the tacit psychological contract; things which would have been taken for granted before.

Today, a lot of benefits that were simply expected and received, without being documented, are being brought into the hiring conversation and incorporated into employment contracts formally. There is a lot more negotiation around terms of employment, and a lot more tailoring and customization.

For managers and organizations alike, that's an added layer of complexity and frustration. On the one hand, employees—and in many cases the law—demand that everyone should be treated equally, and HR departments want everyone on standard contracts and terms; on the other hand, new hires are demanding special treatment and concessions.

And if the company gives way, you have new hires entering the company and receiving special treatment, which causes resentment from longer-serving employees, and from managers who are having to deal with the conflicts and resentment.

And let's not forget the job interview: there, too, the dynamics have changed. In the old model, someone came to a company, and they just wanted to impress the interviewer and get an offer. Today's candidates often view the job interview as a two-way affair, where they are interviewing the employer just as much as they are being interviewed. They are trying to lower the water level on both icebergs: showing who they are and what they want—and what they will give in return—and also trying to get to the core of who this company is that they will be working for, and what the company is going to be willing to give and what they will ask for in return.

Even if nothing ends up documented on paper, it is creating a dialogue and an opportunity to understand each other, and to ensure that that psychological contract stays.

"Yes, you <u>are</u> a number, and no one owes you anything"

It's important to realize you *are* a number, and so is every single member of your team. That sounds incongruous in a book about creating meaningful employee experiences.

Here's what I mean. From the organization's point of view, you are a line on an HR spreadsheet. The company has no idea what's important to you. It has no idea what you want. It has no idea what your boundaries are. So, if you don't know those things for yourself, and if you don't scream them to the rafters, you will just become a number. And when you're just a number, no one owes you anything.

Whether we understood it or not, the psychological contract confirms that we are numbers: it describes the relationship between the organization and *everyone* that works for it. Remember, I said there are no personal psychological contracts; they are collective contracts.

If you think you are anything more than a number, then you are putting too many expectations into that unwritten psychological contract.

At the end of the day, you have an employment contract, in which you are a number. That's a clearer way of saying it.

Anything else is an expectation that can be shattered or met at your manager's whim. It's not written down so nobody can be held to it.

How this helps you manage your team

You have to recognize that expectations exist, whether you like it or not. Knowing that, it is your job to make sure that you and your team members (individually!) are on the same page, and that neither of you is making too many assumptions about the expectations.

The role of the manager has expanded

Life used to be so simple for managers. They would sit down with their peers and set the strategy for their part of the organization. As a Sales Manager, my colleagues and I would create the sales plan for the region, direct the sales representatives, and then measure their call frequency.

VUCA makes the world too complicated for strategy to be set that way. Managers can't have all the answers, but they still worry that they are expected to. That's what they used to do, but now they can't, and as a result, they are feeling overwhelmed and crunched.

The role has expanded, because managers now have to manage and deal with the driving needs of employees. But those needs aren't articulated, and they are infinite and hard to understand. They also have their operational workload piling up on their desk. At the same time, they are trying to keep up with VUCA and understand what is going on in the world. And then there's senior management – it is coming at you from all angles.

As a result, managers are spending less time with people, less time on the human agenda—being collaborative, and trying to build a space of good, healthy collaboration—and instead, they are just scrambling to keep up. They end up focusing on tasks and process because that feels less complex: you can check it off your to-do list, and you feel like you are back in control.

Even when you do find the time to connect with someone, you know that the clock is ticking and you have to hurry up because you both have somewhere else to be.

There is a trend towards flatter organizational hierarchies. That brings with it wider spans of control. Where a manager might once have had 6-8 direct reports, they are now managing 12-14 people, and those people might be distributed globally rather than sitting in the same office. That reduces the time available for direct contact and makes schedules harder to coordinate.

The problem is that relationships need time to be nurtured, and it's hard to find that time. In our old-world, industrialized, performance-focused mindset, we don't make relationships a priority. Even if we want to, we feel too overwhelmed to even find the time. But we need to make time. According to Gallup[6], the most important relationship you have (at work, anyway!) is with your manager. That, if nothing else, deserves time, focus and attention.

---

[6] *State of the American Manager: Analytics and Advice for Leaders. (2015) Gallup.*

At one point in my career, I was managing 15 people, and I was finding it hard to give everybody the time I wanted to, and the time they needed. As a result, I was starting to feel disconnected.

I asked myself, *"How can I honestly provide support for them, or be a good manager when I hardly get to spend time with them, and I'm stuck in these other meetings?"*

The standard way to run a team like mine was to spend a day, or even two, with each team member in the field to fully evaluate how they were doing.

I had an inherent belief that if I wanted them to trust me, I had to find ways to spend time with them, but there weren't enough days in the month to manage that many people the "traditional" way.

Rather than ask them to change how they were working with me, I changed how I was working with them. Instead of spending a full day with each of them individually, I set up two drop-in days each month when I would be available for them to come to me.

The impact on performance was astonishing. When I took over the team, it was one of the worst performing teams in the region. Within nine months, we were in the top six (of twenty-six) teams and won a top performer trip.

People need to be heard

Employees are afraid to voice their needs. They are afraid to speak up for fear of being seen as different, being laughed at, and not being heard. They are too scared to acknowledge that they are human and that they want their employer to actually care about them. It's not that employees are looking for a big heart and a hug from the organization. They just want to feel valued.

In this age of VUCA, we need what they have to offer. Each individual can contribute great perspective, and as we move to a more team-based organization, everybody has to pull their weight in different ways.

It pays to remember that the lower an employee is in the corporate hierarchy, the closer they tend to be to the customer or the outside world. That's where the value lies in the information they bring: they are the ones talking to customers every day; they are the ones who are seeing what's happening; they are probably more connected to competitors than the senior leaders are.

Part of the problem is that lower level employees worry that they are not as articulate as senior leaders, and they aren't as concise in their communication. Leaders have to learn to listen to employees differently from how they listen to other leaders and managers.

We also have to go to them and ask for the information, rather than just waiting for them to come to us. "Sit and wait" worked when the world changed slowly and we had time to react to what was happening. In the world of VUCA, if you wait for an employee to summon up the courage to tell you something is going wrong, you'll run out of time before you even realize what's happening.

How do I know whether my team is holding back?

As a manager, how can you know if your team is holding back? If there is something you need to know about that isn't being said?

One early warning sign is when you are feeling exasperated, and you don't understand why your team doesn't see a situation the way you see it. That suggests they know something you don't.

As Patrick Lencioni points out in *The Five Dysfunctions of a Team*[7], when a team is functioning really well—when people feel safe enough to bring up conflict, discuss, and openly air different opinions—you'll have good dialogue, and you will at least feel heard and listened to. But when you, as a leader, feel frustrated—when it feels like you have to do everything on your own, and no one understands—and you feel alone on your own little island, you need to ask yourself whether the problem is with your team or (more likely) with you. Are you talking *with* them or *at* them?

Another warning signal is when there is no conflict or disagreement at all in your meetings; when people respond "OK" automatically without engaging in a dialogue. If your team members are *yes people*, they are less likely to bring you bad news or engage in healthy conflict.

---

[7] The Five Dysfunctions of a Team: A Leadership Fable, April 11, 2002, by Patrick M. Lencioni

Opening up dialogue

If you're worried that dialogue has closed down and you and your team may not be getting all the information you need, all is not lost.

You need to build trust into your relationships: don't assume it is there!

It can start with short bouts of listening. You don't need to sit everyone down for an hour-long conversation every week: just make time each week to meet one-on-one with your team members to connect and listen.

Of course, you can't just walk in and demand to be told what's going on. You need to build up trust with your direct reports, and as Stephen Covey says in *The Speed of Trust*[8], trust is like a bank account: you have to put the coins of trust in before you can get trust back. How you build up that balance of trust is by just spending a little time each day, or even each week, with someone.

Trust is also built by asking people for their input and opinion, and listening to it and acknowledging it. You don't necessarily have to agree with it or act on it, but you do have to show that you value it.

If someone challenges something you said in a meeting, acknowledge them at the end and thank them: it's likely that challenge led to a far richer discussion than would have been

---

[8] The SPEED of Trust: The One Thing that Changes Everything by Stephen M.R. Covey, February 5, 2008

possible if everyone had just kept quiet and nodded in blind obedience.

When you call out those behaviours, it sets the tone for future meetings. If a team member sees someone else open up and challenge you, and you show appreciation rather than resistance and annoyance, they are more likely to open up themselves in another meeting.

Ultimately, it's about admitting that you don't have all the answers and showing vulnerability. Share examples of mistakes you've made and reward people for speaking up. That is critical. As a manager, I made that sharing part of our team process. During our weekly 30-minute performance huddle, we had two minutes in which somebody had to share a mistake they had made that week, and what they learned from it. At first, the team couldn't see the point, but they quickly shifted and had no problem sharing. The turning point was when they realized that what was important wasn't the mistake, but rather what they did with it and what the outcome was. From then on, we all learned from it and made decisions more quickly.

With Trust Comes Speed

When problems arise, you need to be able to discuss and consider different alternatives, and you need diverse opinions.

Establishing trust within your team, and giving people the freedom to share the good and the bad, allows you to be agile. You can collaborate and bring different perspectives into the evaluation. You can weigh benefits and have honest discussions that aren't one-sided.

In a world of VUCA, you have to accept that no one—not even you—has all the answers. You have to be able to draw it out of the collective wisdom of the team.

Summary

❖ The psychological contract is an unwritten set of rules between the employee and the employer, and VUCA has caused it to change.

❖ The iceberg illustration represents how much is hidden by an individual and organization. The lower the waterline, the more they trust each other.

❖ Managers have less time now, making it harder to nurture relationships and keep the waterline low.

❖ Dialogue is key. It builds trust, which gives you speed and accuracy in decision making

PART TWO

The Secret to Success in the New World of Work

We have maxed out on industrial efficiency. Now we must focus on human efficiency, and that means understanding the people in our organizations.

Chapter Five

Maslow Still Matters

How people experience the workplace will
impact how they perform. We need to
understand people's needs and shift the
workplace from mundane transactions to
meaningful experiences.

At the heart of the Purposeful Workplace Experience™ is a simple model that has been a staple of management thinking for almost eight decades. If you've attended leadership training at any point in your career, you were probably taught *Maslow's Hierarchy of Needs*[9] very early on.

These two factors—the age of the model, and the stage of professional development at which it is typically taught—often lead to the model being dismissed as too old fashioned and basic to be relevant to "modern" leadership. The reality couldn't be more different. First, it is a model of what drives human behaviour, and that has changed surprisingly little over millions of years, so a few decades barely register. Second, the simplicity of the model is in its visual appearance.

---

[9] Abraham H. Maslow (1943) "A Theory of Human Motivation", published in Psychological Review 50 (4)

Behind that, though, is a great depth of practical and instantly applicable truth.

Maslow's Hierarchy of Needs: a quick refresher

In case your memories of Maslow are in the dim and distant past—or you've never heard it before—let me give you a quick summary of the model. Even if you know (or you think you know) the model, it's worth revisiting it.

Now, this isn't a full explanation of the model, simply a very high-level introduction, but at its core, Maslow's hierarchy is a visual depiction of five levels of needs that humans strive for in their life (Figure 3).

1. Physiological

2. Safety

3. Belonging

4. Esteem

5. Self-Actualization

Within that, in Figure 3, I have classified those five needs as either *Base Needs* or *Higher Needs*. The Base Needs are those which primarily impact our physical wellbeing. The Higher Needs are more concerned with our emotional wellbeing.

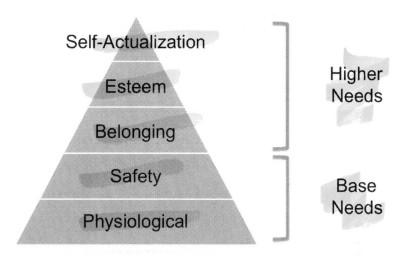

Figure 3: The Hierarchy of Needs

Physiological needs: These are basic requirements for the survival of an organism: food, air, water, clothing, and shelter. The physiological needs have to be met before you can start to think about the next level (Safety). Indeed, that holds true at every level, which is why the model is referred to as a hierarchy: the Base Needs have to be met before you can move to a higher level.

Safety needs: The need to feel safe and secure is another very basic requirement for people to function. It includes both physical and emotional safety. Physical safety is about things like the environment we live in and work in, having a regular paycheque, and living in a society that is governed by the rule of law. Emotional safety comes from knowing that nothing threatens that physical safety: having job security, health coverage, zoning laws, stable government, etc. The insurance industry is built on this safety need: whether it be life coverage, health coverage, or even car or pet coverage, insurance is about ensuring our ability to deal with and recover from setbacks.

Love/Belonging: If you are getting the other two levels of need met, you can move to the next level, which is the need to feel loved or that you 'belong', as well as the need to give love and to make others feel that they belong. We'll discuss this in more depth later, but the key point is that someone who feels their job or financial security is under threat will disconnect from their manager, their team and the company simply because the need for security will take priority over the need to be part of the team or the organization. People who don't feel safe don't make good team players!

Esteem: Esteem refers to the desire to feel that you have status, that you are valued and that you are seen as performing well. It's about having good feelings of self-worth and having self-respect.

The final level is **Self-Actualization:** the idea that you are doing exactly what you should be doing, that you are fulfilling your purpose in life. At this level, everything is coming together, so creativeness can flow out of you.

Now, as I said above, the levels need to be fulfilled in order: you can't move up to the next level until you've fulfilled the levels beneath it. By the same token, if a lower level is knocked out by something that happens, it disrupts everything above it: it doesn't matter how much self-esteem or prestige you have if you haven't got safety.

That's the big challenge from VUCA: the unpredictability and uncertainty threaten those lower levels, especially the need for safety.

Have we seen this somewhere else?

The interesting thing about Maslow is how it relates back to something we saw earlier: the development of the brain.

We said the reptile brain was the first part to develop and governs our survival instincts. That sounds a *lot* like meeting the physiological and safety needs.

Then the mammalian brain developed, which governs emotional responses. That corresponds closely to the belonging and esteem needs.

And finally, the 'human' brain—the logical brain—developed, and indeed, humans are the only species that seek fulfilment and purpose in life.

I also said that the reptile brain calls the shots and nothing else can happen until it's feeling safe, in exactly the same way that we can't focus on higher needs until the lower needs are met.

In other words, Maslow's hierarchy actually corresponds to the way our brains are built.

Maslow and employment

In the first part of this book, we drew a distinction between the formal contract of employment and the unspoken psychological contract between a company and its employees.

On a very transactional level, employment is how people meet their Base Needs: it provides money to feed ourselves and our family, and it provides financial stability. The written employment contract simply sets out in a legally enforceable form how employment will do that.

The psychological contract, on the other hand, is about how people get their higher needs met at work.

Maslow and leadership

Chip Conley makes an interesting observation about Maslow and styles of leadership: "a transactional leader is leading from the bottom of the pyramid while the transformational leader is leading from the top."[10] In other words, transactional leaders focus on Base Needs, while transformational leaders focus on Higher Needs.

In many ways, my experience of Paul's illness was part of my journey to self-actualization. It forced me to start leading from the top rather than leading from the bottom.

One perceived challenge with applying Maslow "in the real world" is that you can't measure it and track it. Even more than that, you can't identify a direct link between Maslow's needs and performance.

What we can show, though, is a connection between engagement and productivity. How does that tie back to Maslow? Well, right in the centre of the hierarchy is "Belonging." So, once we meet the Base Needs of employees, they start to feel

---

[10] Conley, Chip. (2007). *PEAK: How great companies get their mojo from Maslow.* Jossey-Bass

a connection with the company, their colleagues, and their manager. That is the most basic form of engagement.

At the next level—esteem—they are looking for validation and to increase their self-worth, and will seek to perform at a higher level to get that validation and greater self-worth.

And finally, they seek to feel that their work has meaning and purpose—they seek self-actualization.

Workers who are connected, who are striving to work at a higher level, and who find meaning in their day-to-day work—that's a key component of workplace engagement!

If we accept that when people's needs are met, they are more engaged, then we can see a link from meeting those needs to driving higher performance.

Now, it would be easy to fall into the trap of thinking that in a developed, western society people's lowest-level needs are being fulfilled. But remember: the fear of loss disrupts safety needs just as much as actual loss because it takes away the certainty that today's comfortable existence will be in place tomorrow.

In recent years, there have been a number of books that deal with the Higher Needs—for example, Dan Pink's *Drive*[11], which talks about autonomy, mastery, and purpose; or

---

[11] Drive: The Surprising Truth About What Motivates Us, by Daniel H. Pink, April 5, 2011

Simon Sinek's *Start With Why*[12] and Dan Pontefract's *The Purpose Effect*[13], which discuss the importance of purpose—but people are struggling to get there because their safety and belonging needs are being challenged.

Performance happens at the intersection of purpose and belonging

When someone feels like they belong, they feel safer, more confident, and more able to feel vulnerable. Amy Cuddy[14] and Brené Brown[15] both argue that the ability to show vulnerability—to admit that you aren't perfect and make mistakes—is a very valuable leadership quality. You have to be yourself in situations where things can go wrong. You have to take risks. You don't have to be perfect. And it's OK to be vulnerable in front of others—in particular, as Brown points out, you have to be OK with not having all the answers.

A child learns by taking risks and making mistakes. If a child were worried that every time it stumbled and fell it would be punished or that its parents would stop loving it, it would never learn to walk. Adult learning is no different. We can memorize facts and figures by rote, but the only way to gain lessons and learn from experience is to take a risk and to be

---

[12] Start With Why: How Great Leaders Inspire Everyone to Take Action, by Simon Sinek, December, 2009
[13] The Purpose Effect: Building Meaning in Yourself, Your Role and Your Organization May 10 2016 by Dan Pontefract
[14] Cuddy, Amy. (2015). PRESENCE: *bringing your boldest self to your biggest challenges.* Little, Brown and Company
[15] Brown, Brene. (2012). *Daring Greatly: How the Courage to Be Vulnerable Transforms the Way We Live, Love, Parent, and Lead.* S: Avery Publishing Group.

allowed to fail. That means that leaders have to create an environment—a climate—in which it is safe to fail. You can feel you belong when you join a group, but you can really elevate your competence, presence, and influence within that group when you feel safe enough to be vulnerable and fail without fear.

The other side of the equation is *purpose*. Purpose gives you focus and an ability to grow and be creative. The modern workplace is full of distractions, from colleagues walking by in an open plan office and starting a conversation, to the incessant buzzing and beeping of our phones, tablets, and computers to tell you another deadline has arrived or someone is trying to chat.

When someone is working on a task that is 'on purpose' for them, however, they lose themselves in the task. Mihaly Csikszentmihalyi[16] talks about "flow": a state of concentration or complete absorption with the activity at hand and the situation. It is a state in which people are so involved in an activity that nothing else seems to matter.

That ability to focus, and to connect with and find purpose in what you do, allows you to not be distracted and achieve real depth.

---

[16] Csikszentmihalyi, Mihaly (1990). *Flow: The Psychology of Optimal Experience*. New York: Harper and Row

It is the combination of the depth that comes from purpose and the lack of fear that comes from belonging that is magical.

That intersection is a euphoric state when you are fully there. It's not necessarily achievable in all organizations and all situations, but the closer you can help people get there—to feel like they belong and to help them find purpose—the more engaged they will be.

Why personal connection is important

In the last few years, our understanding of the internal workings of the brain has increased radically. In his book *Social*[17], Matthew Lieberman shows that the way our brains are wired to connect is very similar to the mechanisms that drive us to eat, drink, have water, and survive. So, while we might assume that social connection is a 'want', it is actually a 'need'.

We intuitively believe that social and physical pain are radically different kinds of experiences yet the way our brains treat them suggests that they are more similar than we imagine.

"Social" by Matthew Lieberman

So, neuroscience backs up Maslow's assertion that we have a need to connect, to "belong". It also suggests that ignoring social wellbeing is likely to harm team performance, and

---

[17] Lieberman, M. D. (2013). *Social: Why Our Brains Are Wired to Connect.* Oxford University Press

even individual health, for reasons we could not have guessed.

Lieberman's research suggests that when your social bonds are damaged, your brain responds the same way that it does to physical pain.

That makes Maslow's *Belonging* need an interesting crossover. It is tempting to assume that it is one of the Higher Needs, like *Esteem* and *Self-Actualization*. What Lieberman's work is saying, however, is that *Belonging* is a Base Need, more akin to our needs for *Physiological Survival* and *Safety*.

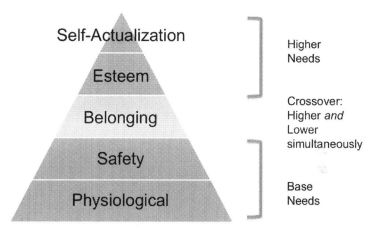

Figure 4: The power of "Belonging"

And yet, *Belonging* <u>does</u> impact emotional well-being significantly. So, we have to think of it as both a Higher Need and a Lower Need at the same time, which is why it's so powerful (Figure 4).

Connecting the dots

Achieving true alignment between the organization and the individual is actually very difficult. In *The Purpose Effect*[18], Dan Pontefract points out that perfect alignment is very rare. What is realistic, though, is to find a connection *somewhere*, some degree of alignment to connect the two. If an employee truly can't connect the two, then you need to think about whether they are in the right role or even company.

In that respect, while finding alignment might, on the surface, appear to be about meeting higher-level, emotional, needs, it also has a major impact on the lower-level, safety needs.

So, as a leader, you have to somehow connect your own purpose, your team's purpose, and the company's purpose, and then help each individual team member to connect their own purpose. That's a lot of connections. Where do you start? And how do you manage it all?

The easiest place to start is with yourself. You need to connect to your own purpose first, and if you can't find it then have someone help you find it, be it a coach, a colleague, or your own manager. But understand the purpose of what you are doing.

Next, you need to help your team members find their own personal purpose. It's not for you to tell them what that

[18] The Purpose Effect: Building Meaning in Yourself, Your Role and Your Organization May 10 2016 by Dan Pontefract

purpose is, as much as you probably would love to, but you have a critical role to play by asking questions.

> One of my direct reports shared that she was bored in her role but didn't want to leave because it gave her a predictable income.
>
> We had a good relationship, so I was aware of her outside interests and long-term ambitions. Instead of directing her, I asked questions to help her connect the current situation to her aspirations.
>
> Taking the time to have that conversation about meaning helped her find purpose in her daily activities. Her performance at work improved, and colleagues commented on her increased level of engagement.

An important point to make here is that purpose doesn't need to be a higher, moral, life-changing purpose. You just need to understand why you are doing what you are doing.

The power of connection

Connection is part of meeting our need for Belonging. It's what pulls you beyond the quest for safety and survival, and elevates you so you're not just living a life of fear.

As Lieberman points out, the human brain is hardwired to belong. It's not conscious, and it's not something we can control: your brain needs to connect with other people.

Employees meet their social needs—the need for belonging—in many ways beyond overtly social activities:

community work, church, family, hobbies. Increasingly, as employees spend more time at work, those needs are being met through employment.

The organization where I worked for many years helped employees connect to a community purpose in two primary ways. At the team level, we would select an activity that benefited the community, or collect money, or organize an event for a charity. That allowed us to connect team and individual purpose. One year, for example, my team spent the day painting a house as part of a Habitat for Humanity project. Another year, we packed medicines for Doctors Without Borders.

At an organizational level, the employees voted to select a "charity of choice" so that our efforts could have a greater impact. This connected us as an organization to a collective purpose, and for many years we helped a national healthcare not-for-profit organization to expand their impact across Canada. In fact, it even led to changes in federal policy.

How to help employees meet their higher needs

When individuals aren't getting their higher needs met, they start to act out and push back. In his books *Juice*[19] and *Beyond*

---

[19] Juice: The Power of Conversation—The Secret to Releasing Your People's Brilliance and Expanding Your Leadership Influence, Revised Edition Jun 6 2012 by Brady G. Wilson

Engagement[20], Brady Wilson points out that employees can let you know that their needs are not being met and that they can attempt to meet those needs in two ways: *skillfully* and *unskillfully*.

For example, if Belonging is really important for you, but it isn't being met at work, you might initiate activities that are more inclusive; try to build opportunities to bring people together; promote a team environment and try and do team activities. That's the *skillful* way to show what's happening. The *unskillful* way would be to create an atmosphere that's cliquey and gossipy.

Ultimately, people are going to have their needs met. The question is whether that is going to be done skillfully or unskillfully. If left too long, then the emotional connection to the company suffers, making it easier for someone to walk away.

That can be a huge loss for a company. When an employee leaves, they're not just taking away their labour. They are taking away the investment you made in training them. They are taking away the store of corporate knowledge and information that they have built up. And they are taking away the relationships—internal and external—that they built up.

---

[20] Beyond Engagement: A Brain-Based Approach That Blends the Engagement Managers Want with the Energy Employees Need   Jun 23 2015 by Brady G Wilson

It's much easier, safer and cheaper to keep hold of your talent by making sure that their needs are being met.

A final thought on Maslow (for now)

Simon Sinek's *Leaders Eat Last*[21] is based on a simple idea: trust and co-operation will build when leaders look out for their employees.

This idea of 'servant leadership' is nothing new. It doesn't mean you need to be a martyr, though. What Sinek is really saying is that you need to make it a priority of yours to ensure that your employees are getting their Higher Needs met.

Here is an interesting corollary to that idea: if a leader is unable to put themselves second, then arguably they are stuck themselves at the bottom of Maslow's hierarchy: they are trying to find security and holding everyone back because they can't get any higher on the hierarchy of needs, even though they are higher in the corporate hierarchy.

---

[21] Sinek, Simon. (2014). *Leaders eat last: Why some Teams pull together and others don't.* Portfolio Penguin

Summary

❖ Maslow's hierarchy of needs is relevant to workplace success. Base needs are safety and physiological. Higher needs are belonging, esteem and self-actualization.

❖ Chip Conley's perspective that transactional leaders lead from the base needs and transformational leaders lead from the higher needs continues to hold true in today's VUCA environment.

❖ Performance happens at the intersection of purpose and belonging. Purpose gives people a reason to perform and our brains are wired to belong and connect with others.

Chapter Six

"Experiences" Aren't Just for Customers

Looking at a situation through a different lens will often uncover new perspectives. Understanding how the business is operating through the eyes of employees will lead to valuable insights.

Marketers have been using "customer experiences" to increase loyalty and drive profits for several years now. Transferring this concept into the workplace is simply common sense. Josh Bersin[22] and Jacob Morgan[23] have both written extensively about the employee experience, and I agree wholeheartedly with their perspective. Organizations need to look at creating employee experiences first, and that will translate into positive customer experiences.

Let's start by thinking about what marketers mean when they use those terms about customers.

---

[22] *Global Human Capital Trends 2016: The new organization, different by design. Deloitte University Press*
[23] *Morgan, J. (2017). The employee experience advantage: how to win the war for talent by giving employees the workspaces they want, the tools they need, and a culture they can celebrate. Hoboken, NJ: Wiley*

The *customer experience* is everything that happens in the interactions between an organization and its customers over the length of their relationship. It determines how the customer feels about your company and your products or services, and sets the tone for the relationship between you.

Understanding that customer experience helps you to in turn deepen your understanding of the customer so you can create products or services to alleviate a specific pain point that they are having.

McDonald's managers, for example, walk the customer journey for their own store every day. They start a few hundred yards away from their restaurant, walk to it the way a diner would, stand in line with the customers, order a meal, wait for it, collect it and then walk out of the restaurant and down the street. All that time, they are looking at the world through the customer's eyes, understanding what it's like to be a customer, and looking for opportunities to improve the experience.

The traditional way companies and employees interact

Traditionally, companies haven't looked at the employment transaction in the same way that they look at selling a product or service. The power has been with the organization, and the employee is there to meet the needs of the organization. The attitude was very much that the employee was lucky to be allowed to work for the company.

There was a time and place for that, but—as I outlined earlier—the world has changed. Just as with the psychological contract, the balance of power is shifting. The employee is looking to get something out of the relationship, too.

Companies that are already thinking ahead are now talking in terms of an *Employee Value Proposition* (EVP) alongside their customer value proposition: what is the benefit to you (the employee) of working for us (the employer)?

You can no longer assume that an employee will work out for themselves all the benefits of working for you. Indeed, smaller and newer companies can now compete directly in the employer stakes with older, larger, more established companies. So, now you have to go out of your way to advertise the benefits of choosing you as an employer, and you have to build a real connection. When you reach out and connect with a potential employee and say, *"Hey, here's what we can offer you,"* you are, in effect, saying, *"We are interested in you,"* and starting to shift the power structure.

As I said in Chapter 4, the employment interview itself is changing. Employees are now asking questions about what it will be like to work for the company. They are interviewing their prospective employer to understand what the employee experience will be like there.

> A former colleague of mine, Trish, took a job with a company even though she had been warned by various people that her new boss was difficult to deal with. Trish ignored the warnings and, sure enough, it was a horrible employee experience.
>
> The manager would call her at all hours—once, even at one o'clock in the morning—and didn't respect professional boundaries with her. Trish came close to walking out but didn't because she wanted the security and financial stability the job gave her.

When she finally did apply for a new job at a different company, she made a point of interviewing the employer. I asked her why she hadn't done that the last time around. "I never thought I needed to," she said, "but I made sure I did it this time, because I wasn't going to make the same mistake again!"

If we take that experience concept and move it to employees, we have to let go of thinking of employment as a transaction or a set of contractual obligations.

What I'm talking about is not just a matter of understanding how your employee feels today, tomorrow or yesterday; it is understanding the experience they have with the company from the moment they read about you on a website or in a recruitment ad, or hear about you from a friend, all the way through their daily interactions during their employment, and beyond that to what happens when their employment ends and after they leave.

That's an exercise you can't do on paper or in your head: just like a McDonald's manager, you have to walk it, experience it, and document it.

The employee experience and the customer experience are really about increasing loyalty and trust.

When you plan and manage the employee experience, it deepens the connection: you develop an emotional tie, and it helps you build trust and retain the employee. Just as customers buy from suppliers they know, like and trust, employees want to be hired by companies they know, like and trust, and they want to work for organizations they know, like and trust.

More and more, these days, you also see employees who don't actually intend to change jobs looking at the job market and going to interviews with other companies. They are testing the market, seeing what's out there and listening to what other companies have to say. Essentially, they are exploring what the employee experience is like elsewhere.

As an employer, if you're serious about creating a compelling employee value proposition, you should welcome this, not fear it. If someone comes to you and says they could get certain benefits by going to another company, take that as an opportunity to improve the employee experience.

And if you are confident that your EVP is already excellent, let them go and test the waters, because you know they'll come back.

How do Employees experience your organization?

Paying attention to the employee experience gives you a holistic, more diverse viewpoint, and opens your mind to a wider range of opinions and options you may not have considered. Especially if you've been working for the company yourself for a long time, market norms have probably changed so it can be beneficial to get some feedback on how you treat your employees.

You have to look at the organization through the eyes of your employees. Understanding the employee experience starts with mapping out the employee journey. It doesn't have to be complicated, but it is important to map it out visually, not just as text.

Make sure you address the whole process, rather than an individual interaction or transaction. Then, you can dive deeper into thinking about each of the day-to-day touchpoints that happen along that journey.

Many internal processes are designed for the convenience of the organization, and it shows: how can we maximize control? How can we maximize efficiency? How can we minimize the number of employees in this? Remember, instead, to look at this from the employee's point of view.

Your employees are the ones using the processes, tools, and systems. It's important to understand the impact—good and bad—upon them. When you understand how your employees are experiencing the workplace, you can start to make small, continuous improvements, just as you would with an operational process.

The employee journey and performance

About six to nine months after being hired, the employee is getting into a performance cycle: contributing to business objectives, getting recognition, and setting their own goals.

At the same time, the employee is learning, growing and achieving satisfaction. Developmental opportunities start to open up to them: coaching; training; they may become part of succession planning.

Part of this performance cycle is also the relationships the employee has, with their co-workers and with their manager and the company leadership.

This performance cycle is where creating a Purposeful Workplace Experience™ can have the biggest impact, because it increases momentum in that performance and growth cycle and keeps people from leaving. It is about building trust and sustaining relationships through the performance and growth cycles so that when something unpredictable happens, you have already built that foundation that will help people to continue to perform through times of uncertainty, turmoil and—often—intense emotions.

Some organizations are looking for ways to extend this performance cycle by conducting "stay interviews" with staff alongside exit interviews. Companies are used to the idea of interviewing staff who are leaving to discover what prompted that decision. The stay interview turns that idea on its head by getting the views of staff who are not leaving about what makes them want to stay: Why are they proud to work at a place? What are the factors keeping them there? It's an important part of the journey to understand.

You are part of their Experience too!

Think about how your direct reports feel when they see your name in their Inbox or when your name flashes up on their phone. Are they happy to see it's you, or do they immediately think "Oh ****, what have I done now?" These are microinteractions.

Start to think about the small microinteractions on a regular basis rather than simply thinking about the 'big' moments twice a year. All those microinteractions will add up and impact the employee experience. They seriously impact your credibility and can put Trust Coins in that account I mentioned in Part One.

Summary

❖ The balance of power is shifting from employers to employees who want clarity on what's in it for them to work at your company.

❖ Looking at the employee journey in your organization gives you new perspective and will contribute to the development of an Employee Value Proposition (EVP).

❖ Leaders impact the employee experience through microinteractions and these interactions add up so it is important to make each one count.

Chapter Seven

Redefining Productivity

The new reality of work requires a new
definition of productivity—something
broader, that addresses the human aspects of
work, not simply the mechanical aspects.

I want to introduce you to the idea of *emotional productivity*
in contrast to the kind of productivity leaders are usually concerned with, which we can call *industrial productivity*.

The industrial mindset effectively holds that if a job takes
one person ninety days to complete, then you should be able
to get ninety people to do it in one day or—as more often
happens—you can give one person forty-five days to do it
and they just need to be twice as productive to get it done on
time.

It's a faulty logic that assumes people are just machines that
happen to be made of flesh and blood; that we are driven by
rewards and punishment; and that there is a linear
relationship of performance to some motivational factor and,
as long as we can find that factor, we can achieve anything
we want.

Ultimately, it is our minds, not our bodies, that determine
our ability to produce. Your body might be able to do one

thing, but the mind and body are connected, and your brain will shut down your industrial productivity outside of your conscious control unless you take steps to maintain your emotional productivity.

Emotional productivity is built on human needs, not on robotic needs. We are not machines that can be started and will just keep going until someone flicks the off switch.

What do I mean when I say that "emotional productivity is built on human needs"? I mean that we have to keep Maslow in mind at all times. You can't just work people into the ground and ignore whether their needs are being met. In the short term, you'll reach a level of industrial productivity, but you are incurring a massive opportunity cost, and your team could be far more productive if you didn't ignore their needs.

The same applies to you: you can drive yourself hard and tell yourself you need to get the task done at all costs, but your productivity will drop and, eventually, you will burn out.

I'm not saying that leaders need to be hostage to everyone's needs. You don't have to pander to them and treat them with kid gloves. But you do have to recognize that those needs exist and that if you don't pay attention to them and watch for the signs of burnout, your productivity will suffer. You'll feel productive because things are getting done, but you might only be working at 40% productivity.

It's tempting to ignore these needs. In business, measurement is key: we like things we can track and measure. What I'm talking about here is how people feel about the way you're driving them. That's hard, if not impossible, to measure.

Cognitive (Over)load

The brain uses energy disproportionately: it consumes 80% of the energy used by your entire body. A lot of that energy is used in decision-making: each time you have to make a choice or pick a position, your energy supply is reduced. It's known as "cognitive load': the cost of having to apply your brain to a problem.

Think of the numerous problems you are facing on a daily basis. Your energy reserves are not infinite. They get depleted, which in turn means that your brain has a finite capacity to make decisions.

People are constantly being forced to make decisions; more of them every day. It's exhausting, and once your energy is depleted, the ability for your brain to make decisions (also called executive functioning) is seriously compromised.

That is *cognitive overload*: the situation where you're forcing your brain to make more decisions and use more energy than it is physically capable of. It's not a matter of intellect or skill: it's simple mechanics.

This is something that is easy for leaders to overlook: we think people are making decisions and things are getting done (industrial productivity). You believe they're being productive, but the quality is not what it could be, and everyone is too exhausted and too caught up in their own whirlwind of decisions and challenges to notice (emotional productivity).

> One day, I was sitting in my home office writing a coaching letter with my feedback to one of the sales representatives I had worked with that day. Normally,

> it would take me ten minutes to get one of those let-
> ters out. That day, I sat there for two hours.
>
> I had felt tired and not as sharp as usual, but I assumed
> it was because I had two children under four and a ter-
> minally ill husband. I thought I was just "a little over-
> tired."
>
> Less than a month later, a former boss (who was also
> a good friend) took me out to lunch. She said she had
> something important to discuss with me. Little did I
> know it was an intervention!
>
> I was convinced I was fine, but after my lunch with her,
> I realized I wasn't. I broke down and agreed I needed
> time off to recover.

There are a lot of people operating in a haze at work. Their emotional productivity is virtually zero. It is hard to be productive when you can't think straight. You make decisions on autopilot simply because your boss has told you that you have to come up with a decision by the end of the day: it's safer to make *any* decision than to wait and think clearly.

The role of the leader

We have already seen that people are overwhelmed and exhausted and are trying to find purpose and belonging. In that context, what is the role of the leader?

First, you need to step back and recognize the impact you are having. Recognize that, by the very fact that you work in a hierarchy, your actions will have an impact, whether you like it or not. Your job as a leader is to create an environment that facilitates performance; to remove the barriers that hinder performance and productivity. This is starkly different from a manager who optimizes efficiency and productivity.

Are you finding ways to help your employees think and be creative or are you adding to the chaos?

Remember the lowest levels of Maslow's hierarchy: the safety and security needs. *Psychological* safety is as important a component of this as *physiological* safety is *psychological* safety. And you can't simply assume that people will feel safe just because they have a contract of employment with clear terms and conditions. If the culture of the organization is broken, it can quickly erode any sense of safety.

That brings us back to the quote from Chip Conley in Chapter 6 that "a transactional leader is leading from the bottom of the pyramid while the transformational leader is leading from the top." Transactional leaders use the promise of fulfilling those lower needs—or the threat of taking them away—to manage performance. Transformational leaders ensure that the Base Needs are taken care of, whatever else may happen, so that they can focus on driving performance through fulfilling the Higher Needs.

Our second priority has to be to give people time to think. It's not about slowing down—it's about helping people to reflect, think, and use the power of their minds. It's about helping them to manage the endless distractions—which starts with you not adding to the distractions.

It is important to measure productivity from an efficiency perspective: tracking "what" is getting done. At the same time, however, we need to consider "how" that productivity is happening: what is happening that makes people productive (or not)? Their Experience contributes to their productivity.

Summary

- ❖ Industrial productivity focuses on tasks and efficiency. Most organizational measures have focused here.
- ❖ Emotional productivity means focusing on the human needs first as they will influence how everything else gets done.
- ❖ Cognitive overload is rampant in the workplace greatly impacting both types of productivity.
- ❖ Shifting to an experience mindset at work focuses on employee needs and leads to emotional productivity, which unlocks employee potential.

Chapter Eight

Making the Intangible Tangible

Organizational culture is challenging to
understand and even harder to measure.
Despite decades of study, there is no
agreement on how to cut through the
complexity and track the results. In this
chapter, I introduce The Purposeful
Workplace Experience to help you monitor
your culture.

As a leader, it is critical that you pay attention to culture.

Over the last five years, the Global Human Capital Trends
Report[24] has consistently identified culture as an emerging
area of importance for CEOs. Interestingly, however, even
though it is one of the top priorities, the same report highlights that only 20% of CEOs feel they understand it. CEOs
know it's important, but they have no idea what to do about
it. Why? Because it's too intangible and hard to understand.

Now, the idea of corporate culture isn't new. It was first
studied in the 1930s, in an attempt to understand how the
work environment impacts productivity. So organizations
have had decades to think about culture. And yet, 80% of
CEOs of large organizations—as Deloitte points out—don't

---

[24] Rewriting the rules for the digital age: *2017 Deloitte Global Human
Capital Trends, page 30*

know what to do about it. And smaller and medium-sized businesses—companies with fewer resources and fewer people—are five to six years behind those larger organizations. They are only now becoming aware that culture affects them too, and they need to pay attention to it.

That growing awareness of culture is driven by the trends I identified in the earlier parts of this book: globalization, technology, demographics, and the rise of VUCA.

Leaders finally realize that, as organizations become less predictable and stable, you can't control things in the same ways they always have.

What is "Culture"?

The challenge for leaders is that "culture" is hard to define concretely and, as I said above, harder to measure. On one—very superficial—level, it is *how things are done around here.* It has also been referred to as *the glue that keeps the organization together,* or *the moral compass.*

Earlier in the book, I showed a pyramid that represents, neatly, the organization's culture (which I've reproduced in Figure 5). The pyramid is divided into multiple layers.

At the top, we have **Behaviours** (what we do) and **Processes** (how we do it). These are the visible aspects of culture: the things we can observe directly. They generate the **Results** that the organization produces.

Then you'll notice a line, which I call the **Trust Boundary**. This represents the limits of what people and organizations are willing to openly share.

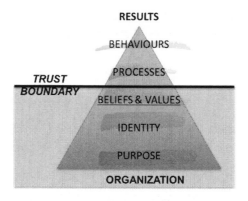

Figure 5: Organizational Culture

Anything above the line is open and visible. Look at any organization, and it's easy to see their processes at work, the behaviours of its employees, and the results the organization creates.

Below the Trust Boundary are things that are harder to observe directly. Organizations may discuss and publish the things below this line—Values and Beliefs, Identity, Purpose—but we can't see them directly.

In exactly, the same way, individuals have a Trust Boundary, which we'll discuss later in this chapter.

I call the line the Trust Boundary for a simple reason: the more open and trusting the relationship you have with someone, the more willing you are to move the Trust Boundary and reveal things that would normally be hidden.

While many aspects of culture are invisible and unstated (behind the Trust Boundary), there are many physical aspects that stare us in the face—the layout of stores or offices; the furniture, art and architecture; office dress codes; the relative position of different employees' parking spaces (or even who has a reserved space and who doesn't); the existence or absence of an executive washroom or cafeteria; even the language people use internally and with customers—but can sometimes be hard to understand or rationalize.

These visible aspects of the culture reflect what is happening behind the scenes, and in particular, the **Beliefs and Values** that run through the organization.

In a very real sense, Values are the building blocks of the visible aspects of culture: they directly drive the behaviours that we see from day to day. Edgar Schein—who is seen as the "grandfather" of organizational culture—made an interesting distinction between *espoused* values and those which are *enacted*.

Espoused values are declared publicly and documented in, for example, a mission statement or values statement. They are being actively championed by senior leadership, but there's always a possibility that the organization is only paying lip service to them. So, alongside the espoused values, we can also think about the *enacted* values: the ones that actually do guide the day-to-day behaviour of people in the company.

In Spring, 2017, United Airlines (strapline "Fly the friendly skies") found itself embroiled in a public relations nightmare after repeated incidents where employees behaved in ways that seemed at odds with its shared (i.e., espoused) values, which included phrases like "warm and welcoming", "doing things the right way", and "delivering on our commitments" (which included a commitment to "make every flight a positive experience for our customers").

From passengers being dragged off planes to aircraft being cleared to fly without proper safety checks, the misalignment between what the airline claimed to be, the standards it invited the public to hold it to, and the behaviours it actually exhibited was jarring.

Underpinning these values and beliefs—and well behind the Trust Boundary—are the deeper aspects of corporate **Identity** (who we are as an organization) and **Purpose** (why the company exists). These are the core underlying assumptions of the organization—usually unconscious and taken for granted by most members of the organization. Here, also, you find the stories that are told within the company: about how it was started, about how "things" work (for example, how people "really" get promoted or offered opportunities), and so on.

Holding all these layers together, and shaping them, is the intricate network of relationships that connects everyone in the organization to everyone else, and to the outside world.

The key defining point of culture is that it is *shared*. You can't have personal cultures: that's just personality (and some personalities are quirkier than others, and some fit better within the organization's culture than others). In that respect, culture is about the shared beliefs, values, understandings and perspectives held by all the employees in your company. It fosters a collective behaviour that really determines how employees get things done.

Is Your Culture Thriving or Declining?

How can you tell the difference between great and not-so-good cultures? The most obvious clue would be one of alignment. Remember I said above that there can be a mismatch between the espoused values and the enacted values; in other words, between how a company says it is going to act and how it actually does act. Similarly, values, processes, and behaviours can be out of line with the core assumptions—for example, when an organization loses sight of why it was started, and what the founders were trying to achieve.

In an organization with a thriving culture all of those elements of culture are fully aligned (Figure 6).

Figure 6: Differences in Organizational Culture

So, in a company with a thriving culture what the company does in the real world matches what it says it will do on paper. That creates a strong corporate identity that is aligned with the organizational purpose: the company is visibly the sort of organization that it says it is.

Such an organization is built on strong trust-based relationships that make healthy, robust conflict possible.

Misalignment happens for three main reasons, and it is usually driven from the top.

First, senior leaders can unwittingly demonstrate behaviours that are incongruent with the espoused values. Why would they do that? Well, VUCA can be a major factor when it pushes us into reactive mode. Incongruent behaviour erodes trust and makes it OK for others in the organization to ignore the culture that leaders are trying to build.

Now, that's about momentary lapses. The second reason for misalignment is when those lapses become the norm; when employees at lower levels don't see senior leaders living the espoused values on a day-to-day basis. For example, the company champions openness, but decisions happen behind closed doors.

And finally, it happens when the company's processes drive a completely different set of behaviours. For example, we may say that we are "putting customers first," but if pay and promotion are based on cost-cutting, and customer satisfaction isn't even tracked, behaviour is never going to support that value.

You have to practice what you preach. If you tell people "This is how we're going to behave," and then you do something that is against the organizational culture, you can't be surprised if everyone else follows suit.

The human dimension

Of course, just as organizations have a culture that drives their *way of being*, so the employees within those organizations have their own way of being. And, just like organizational culture, we can show that way of being as a pyramid (Figure 7).

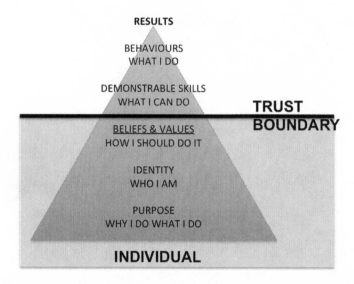

Figure 7: The individual's way of being

So, individuals have a sense of personal **Purpose**; an idea of the kind of person they are (their **Identity**); **Beliefs and Values** that guide their idea of right and wrong, good and bad; they have **Skills** and knowledge and abilities; and they put those skills and knowledge and abilities into practice through their **Behaviours**. Those behaviours create specific **Results**.

Line up, Line up!

In an ideal world, the organization's pyramid and the pyramid of every individual in the organization would be perfectly aligned, where the tips of the triangles (results) rest on each other. To make that easier to visualize, let's turn the organizational culture on its head (Figure 8).

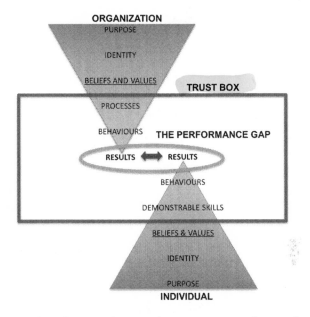

Figure 8: Misalignment between the organization and its employees

When we do this, we can see that the Trust Boundary now becomes a Trust <u>Box</u>. Everything that is within that box is visible and open. As I said earlier, trust moves the boundary: the more trust there is in a relationship, the more that Trust Box opens up. More specifically, what opens up that box is trust, transparency, and authenticity.

We also see that there is now a Performance Gap since the triangles aren't resting on each other. That gap arises because the results an employee is generating aren't aligned with the results the organization needs.

Individual results ultimately drive the organization's results, and the individuals' speed and efficiency determine the organization's speed and efficiency, so the greater that gap is, the less efficient and productive the organization and its employees become.

Also, the greater the distance between the tips of the two triangles——the harder it is for that employee to fit in, to engage meaningfully with their job, their team and the company, and ultimately even to deliver on their roles and responsibilities satisfactorily. The closer the two tips are, the more the individual will be able to generate the kinds of results the organization expects from them. Closing the gap also makes the environment less frustrating for the employee and adds to their resilience.

In reality, of course, it's almost impossible to achieve 100% alignment between the organizational culture and every single employee's personality. If you did, you would have an army of clones, not a team. But, you can aim to minimize the size of the disconnect.

From Performance Gap to Personal Disconnect

Just like an organization, the different aspects of the individual can also get out of alignment. For example, an individual may hold one set of values. If the organizational culture demands that they behave in a way that conflicts with those values, either because the organization's values (espoused or enacted) conflict with their own, or because processes and reward structures are driving them to do things they are not comfortable with, that will have serious implications for the employee. That is how disconnect starts. And, of course, it goes without saying that the forces of VUCA challenge alignment. VUCA pushes both the organization and the individual, and can widen the gap (Figure 9).

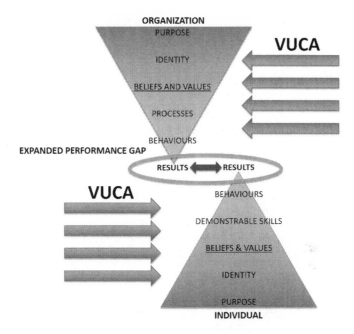

Figure 9: VUCA widens the Performance Gap

Once the performance gap hits a certain length, the individual will feel stressed and overwhelmed. The source and nature of that stress and overwhelm depend on where they are in terms of meeting their needs.

Someone who is fairly fulfilled, and is focusing on their Higher Needs, will see the misalignment as a conflict between their self-esteem and self-actualization—their ability to 'be themselves' at work—and their need to belong. Taking a stand against what they are being asked to do creates the risk of being ostracized by their peers and boss, so they face a daily choice between being true to themselves and being loyal to their friends and colleagues.

Someone who is focused on the lower-level, safety and security needs will worry that taking a stand could cost them their job. They face a daily choice between being true to themselves and feeding their family.

Either way, if they continue to act as expected—if they allow themselves to toe the company line and align themselves with the organizational culture—they are going to feel unfulfilled, stressed, and inauthentic (Figure 10).

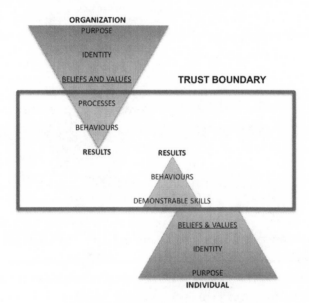

Figure 10: How disconnect starts

You are creating mechanical robots who do your bidding without question. The problem is, those kinds of employees typically don't care much about the organization (it's forcing them to act out of character) or about its customers. PR disasters like United Airline's headline-grabbing events are the most obvious manifestation of that disconnect, but the damage can be more subtle, building up day by day to the full disconnect I discussed in Part 1.

From Disconnection to Full Dysfunction

The nightmare scenario is when you combine misalignment in the individual and the organization; when you have a group of people who are forced to act against their own character in pursuit of the objectives of an organization that has lost its way (Figure 11). The end result is poor relationships, low trust, and frustrated employees. That, in turn, leads to low profitability and poor employee engagement scores (assuming, of course, that you've been tracking employee engagement!).

Of course, the outcome of these misalignments doesn't have to be criminal. More often, the consequences are simply the heavy toll taken on everyone in the organization.

For an organization, this is the top of a slippery slope to scandal and a very real risk of collapse. This is how a reputable firm like Arthur Andersen ends up shredding incriminating documents to cover up internal fraud at Enron. This is how a respected car manufacturer like Volkswagen starts to install software designed to create false emissions readings. This is how a global giant like Toshiba ends up overstating its earnings by $Billions over a period of seven years.

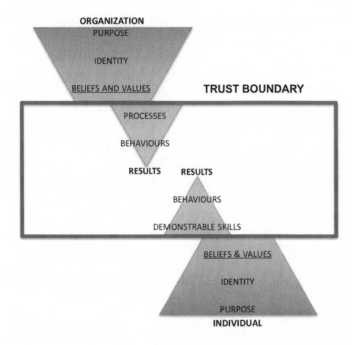

Figure 11: Full dysfunction

Why the leader needs to define culture

It's easy to assume that culture is something that just evolves over time; that it *records* how people act rather than *defining* it; that you hire people and what emerges as they interact with each other and with the outside world is a company culture.

It's easy to assume that CEOs only really create the culture when the company is small and revolves around them.

It is easy, but it is a mistake.

The CEO is instrumental in creating the culture of an organization. The truth is that if, as a leader, you don't actively monitor and shape the culture of the organization, it will shape itself, and it will be modelled on what you *do* not what you *say*.

> One of my clients was the CEO of a medium-sized company. She was worried because her team was working extremely long hours. If someone asked someone else to do something, they would just do it; no one said "no" to any requests.
>
> That wasn't the environment she wanted to create. The way she saw it, it was OK for her to work long hours and constantly add things to her workload, because she was the CEO, and it was what she expected of herself. But she didn't want her team to feel under pressure to act that way.
>
> Of course, the problem was that, however much she might tell them that it was OK to say no and to go home on time, her actions said otherwise. She had no idea that her behaviour had such a strong and counter-productive influence on the company's culture.

Culture can be both a risk and an asset to your business. You need to take an intentional approach and hire someone with the right expertise to guide you and help you evolve a culture that is a natural fit for what your company needs.

Changing from the middle

I am about to contradict myself. If you're reading this and you're not the CEO, you're probably thinking, "Carolyn said earlier that culture can't change from the middle. So what's the point of me doing *any* of this."

Culture change has to start somewhere, and you can have successful change in the middle or bottom levels, so I don't want to dissuade anyone from creating a more positive environment. In fact, this is where The Purposeful Workplace Experience can start! (More on that shortly).

While culture ultimately starts with the leaders, it can be influenced at all levels. If you work in the knowledge economy, you hire people for their knowledge and critical thinking skills. Leading in that type of workplace is very different and requires unique skills. You have to create an environment that allows knowledge, creativity, and innovation to flow, rather than restricting them.

The danger with starting in the middle—with a single manager or even a group of managers changing the culture of their team or department—is that it can easily be swept aside by a strong CEO, especially if there's a change at the top of the organization. The solution is to make sure that you get senior leaders to buy into what you're doing. Otherwise, it will stick for a while, but ultimately it will be crushed from on high.

So, let's restate Schein's assertion. Culture change cannot *start* in the middle: you have to get support from the top, and then you can *shape it* from the middle.

Using Purposeful Workplace Experience™ to positively shape the culture

There are many approaches to culture change. Let's look at how Purposeful Workplace Experience™ is different.

The Purposeful Workplace Experience™ is about helping leaders create an environment where they know not only *what* is happening, but also *why* it's happening. And it's a way of understanding what's really happening as compared to what is being reported back to them.

Often, in organizations, there's a reality gap between leaders and employees. Employees are closer to the outside world. They are the ones communicating daily with customers, with suppliers, with partners. Senior leaders get a heavily sanitized version of that. Managers report to them, but—at least in a typical, non-Purposeful Workplace Experience™ workplace—they make sure that the messages are close to what they think their boss wants to hear. It's a simple survival strategy, but it means that senior leaders are often disconnected from the reality of what is happening outside the cocoon of the boardroom.

Culture change programs can be heavily process-driven. They often focus on fixing processes or systems without getting at the root cause. My approach looks deeper—beyond the symptoms—at what is currently behind the Trust Boundary. That is where you find the building blocks and the glue of the culture. The Purposeful Workplace Experience™ then puts those blocks together and holds them together in an intentional, designed way, to support increased productivity.

Alignment matters

The other major difference from traditional approaches to culture change is that most of those approaches focus almost exclusively on the organization. The Purposeful Workplace

Experience™ aims to align both the organization and the individual (Figure 12).

Restoring that alignment means that the Purposeful Workplace Experience™ has to look beyond behaviours, processes, and values, to also work on the underlying identity and purpose.

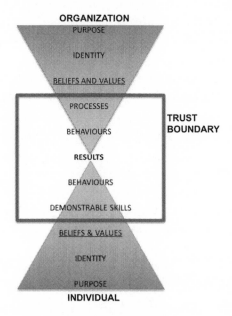

Figure 12: Purposeful Workplace Experience™ restores alignment

When you create that alignment, all the way from organizational purpose through to every individual's personal purpose—and remember, the aim is not perfect alignment, simply to minimize the gap, so that everyone feels that at least their personality is compatible with the organization's culture, and doesn't have to feel to between being themselves and being a 'good' employee—employees feel valued, respected, and heard. The Purposeful Workplace Experience™ then works to maintain that alignment.

Otherwise, VUCA will eventually knock things back out of balance.

That, in turn, results in greater employee engagement, and positive attitudes, thought processes and actions because it ultimately makes the employees feel valued and heard.

Now let's tie that back to what I said earlier. When someone sees their values reflected in the values of the organization, it increases their sense of Belonging. When they are able to do work and generate results that align with their values, it increases their Self-Esteem. And when they see their own purpose reflected in their work and reflected in the purpose of the organization, they are part of something much bigger than themselves—they are closer to achieving Self-Actualization.

That brings us back to the comment I made earlier in this book: transactional leaders manage through the Base Needs; transformational leaders manage through the Higher Needs.

The Purposeful Workplace Experience™ allows employees to reach those Higher Needs of Belonging, Esteem and Self-Actualization.

The Manager Creates a Climate for their Team

Managers have a crucial role to play in whether and how well someone can deal with what is going on. They do it by creating the climate in which their team is operating: the mental and emotional environment that surrounds them every day.

That climate sets the tone for how your team members deal with all the noise, stress and chaos. It determines the skills and behaviours people will display at work. It's the backdrop to everything that happens, so as a leader you want to make sure that everything is fully aligned (Figure 13).

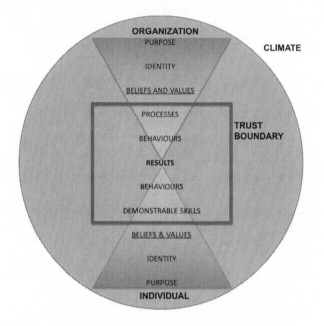

Figure 13: Climate is the backdrop for everything that happens

You can think of VUCA as a force that acts on the two pyramids. VUCA hits the organizational pyramid as big market shifts, and it hits the individual pyramid as big life changes.

If the pyramids are already out of alignment, VUCA can topple one or both of them very easily, or push them even further out of alignment.

When the two pyramids are aligned, they become a much stronger structure together. VUCA may move the structure, but it moves it as a whole: both pyramids move together and stay together.

The Purposeful Workplace Experience establishes conditions for your employees to thrive in. It is the ideal climate to create.

What you need to succeed in this new world of work

In order to get ahead—and to help your team and organization get ahead—in this new world, there are a number of factors and skills you need in place.

First, you need a completely new mindset. Central to this is the recognition that VUCA exists, and it will trash even the most carefully considered strategic plan. To survive VUCA, you have to accept the fact that you can't control everything, and you need to fully trust the people around you.

That starts with a mindset shift about leadership. You need to move away from only managing productivity and KPIs, and start creating space for people to think, innovate and create.

Just like when I was managing 15 employees, you don't have time to be with your team all the time, so you need to be impactful in the time you *do* have. You can have a big impact in small moments.

First, *establish your anchor*. Know who you are and what you want. That starts with defining your purpose: What do you want to achieve? Where are you?

It doesn't have to be a deep philosophical discussion of your life's purpose, but you need to ground yourself in your own sense of identity. VUCA is fast and furious, and if you're not grounded and anchored with something that is meaningful to you, it will blow you over and take you with it. Before you know it, you will be somewhere else, and you won't know how the hell you got there.

> No one understood what it was like living with a dying husband who was in denial. Everybody around me—Paul included—was walking around in an alternate reality, pretending that he wasn't going to die.
>
> Then there was me. I knew my husband was dying, but I didn't want to be negative. Internally, I was in turmoil, but I tried to suppress it. Here was our family with two little boys aged 2 and 3, and a dying father. I wanted to escape and be normal like everybody else.
>
> I knew that the chances of Paul seeing the boys start kindergarten were slim, so I wanted to give him the best possible experience of being a dad. I found a way to buy a new fully detached house—a dream he had always had—and I put all my energy into creating the best possible father and son experiences for him and the boys. I wanted the boys to remember their dad for who he was, not the illness that took his life.

Know your Boundaries

When I talk about boundaries, I mean knowing what you need and what is important to you. So, do you know what your boundaries are? They are defined by your values. Where will you draw the line for working late, taking work home, missing family events or being home in time for dinner. You should at least know where you draw the line. And if you don't set your boundaries, others will set them for you.

They won't do it with bad intent. They probably won't even realize they are doing it. But they will do it.

Use what you have

If there's one thing most managers can depend upon, it is that their budgets will be cut. So we assume that we have less to work with each year. It makes a convenient excuse when targets are missed or results fall.

Start by taking stock of the resources you do have. When you sit back and take stock, you will realize you have more than you realize.

When Paul was diagnosed, I thought to myself, *focus on what you have, not what you don't have, and be grateful.*

I realized that there was no way I would be able to get through the situation alone, so I learned to use the resources around me and reach out for help.

A major resource for me was Hearth Place (their website is Hearthplace.org). It is a physical space, and also a support structure, for families, caregivers, and anyone impacted by cancer. They provide resources and help you through the journey. For Paul and me, the most powerful aspect was the community we became connected to: people following the same journey as us, each at their own pace. The library was useful, as were the patient groups. What made them unique, however, was the connection they created for caregivers, patients, children, and parents of people who were ill, and the collaboration and community that happened.

There were four families in the same position as we were: all with a dying parent, and all with children

> under the age of four. Our children attended a support group together, and the caregivers all attended a separate group together at the same time as the kids were meeting.
>
> We planned to have Christmas parties together, but we only ever got to have one with all the families. The second year, one of the mothers had passed away, so there were only three families. The next year we went down to two, and then there was just us.
>
> Even as members of our circle passed, we would have amazing celebrations each Christmas. My mother couldn't understand it. "There was so much sadness for these families. And yet, when you walked into the room, everyone was enjoying being together. In the midst of all the grief, it was such a wonderful, amazing experience."

A critical step in identifying your resources is tracking what can be controlled and what cannot.

You have control over your attitude, how you want to show up, the quality and quantity of work, whether you attend meetings or not, how serious you are, what you learn, and much more. The reality is, you have control over your time and how you spend it. That's where knowing (and enforcing) your boundaries is critical: will you be a hostage to other people's choices or decisions, or take ownership of your own choices and decisions?

Simply cataloging the aspects you have control over leads you to start making decisions: to allocate your time better, with more intention and purpose, and to set your own boundaries. You start to make intentional decisions about when to delegate, when to do it yourself, and when to push back and say "No."

Think in terms of creating the best conditions you can for the team, and then let their skills go to work!

Do I have a Culture problem?

Look around your organization. Are good, talented people leaving more regularly than you'd like? Are you surrounded by "Yes" people? Are your employee engagement scores dropping lower than your golf handicap? Do employee engagement scores say one thing, but behaviour says something different? Are your customer satisfaction scores dropping? Do things take longer than they should to get done? Are you losing your High Potentials? Do you have a lot of people out on leave?

If you answered yes to any of those, you have a culture that is out of balance and needs help.

TAKE THE QUIZ

Take this quiz to find out how the Purposeful Workplace Experience is showing up at your company.

http://pinnacleculture.ca/questionnaire/

How to start creating a Purposeful Workplace Experience™

Every organizational culture is at risk due to the constant VUCA forces. Therefore, adopting the Purposeful Workplace Experience™ mindset is your best defense. It creates a workplace that helps drive alignment between an individual and their organization and increases the likelihood that the individual will have their needs met at work. It is based on following four simple rules:

- The Rule of Connection: "Connect to people, not process"

- The Rule of Collaboration: "Create opportunities to collaborate, and minimize competition"

- The Rule of Adaptability: "Be adaptable and expect your plans to change"

- The Rule of Equivalence: "Everyone can be a leader if you give them the opportunity"

The extent to which each rule is followed can be represented on a continuum, from something that is never demonstrated to something that is demonstrated all the time, in all situations. Understanding where you are in the continuum of each rule is a useful indicator to assess the state of your culture at that point in time.

In Part Three of the book, we will look at each of those four rules in more detail.

Summary

❖ Culture is hard to measure and has multiple layers, some of which can be observed (behaviors and processes) and some that are not visible (values, beliefs, identity, purpose).

❖ The trust box represents the limits of what people and organizations are willing to openly share.

❖ Values are the building blocks of organizational culture. They include espoused values which are publicly declared and enacted values, which are the ones influencing decisions.

❖ The organizational and individual icebergs should be aligned (tip to tip) to get the highest level of performance. If not, there is a performance gap. Once the gap gets to a certain point, disconnection of the individual occurs and their iceberg becomes misaligned.

❖ Full dysfunction occurs when the organization's iceberg and the individual iceberg are simultaneously misaligned.

❖ A mindset shift about leadership is needed. Think about 'leading through moments'. To have maximum impact in these moments ensure you do the following:
  o Establish your anchor
  o Know your boundaries (which are really values)
  o Uncover and leverage all the resources you can
  o Focus on what you can control

❖ The purposeful workplace experience is the optimal climate a leader can create that will drive alignment between an individual and their organization.

PART THREE

Introducing the Four Rules of Engagement

The world might be complex, volatile and uncertain but you can create predictable patterns of behaviour within your organization.

Chapter Nine

The Rule of Connection: "Connect to people, not process"

Organizations were forced by circumstance to focus on consistency and process, but in the process, they have lost sight of the impact it has on people. You need to connect to people not process and allow yourself to be human because you can only connect when you're being authentic—as one authentic human being to another.

September 2008. Four months before Paul passed away, and five years into his illness. For much of that time, he refused to admit that he was as sick as he was. I think that denial is, in many ways, what kept him alive for as long as it did.

For most of his illness, I focused on Paul and his family, and on connecting with everyone so that we could all experience his shortened time with us in a positive, fun way.

Four months before he passed away, however, my focus shifted. Paul was Catholic, and I wasn't. I have very clear ideas about what I want on my death, which includes being cremated. Paul continually said he wanted that as well. However, knowing this would not be aligned to his Catholic upbringing, I pushed the conversation.

I started to get obsessive about it. In part, I just wanted him to make the decision that was right for him, but he needed to admit he was dying first, and that wasn't easily done.

The cancer had spread to his brain and bones, and he had already changed a lot in the preceding twelve months, so I was worried that I wasn't going to be able to honour his true wishes; that he would be making the decision based on what I or somebody else told him. I wanted it to be his decision.

So, that September, Paul and I were with our counsellor, Scott. Paul looked at me, raised his voice angrily, and asked, "Why do you want me to die?"

I couldn't believe it! I said, "Oh my God! I don't want you to die. I don't want you to die at all."

At that moment, I realized I had become so focused on the process of the funeral that had I lost sight of the impact my questions were having on him, and it had alienated him. My intent was good, but it was destroying him.

Being driven by process can unknowingly impact the people around you negatively—whether at home or at work. I know this is an extreme example, but the point is I had shifted my focus away from people and onto the process: the process of the funeral.

Process is not the same as productivity

As the research shows, productivity is through the floor, and yet all we do is introduce more processes and controls that measure how much worse things are getting, without solving the problem.

It's a natural reaction: "Performance is suffering, so we obviously need to measure it better." But we're not fixing the root cause, which is that people aren't connected to anything or anyone. We are not giving ourselves a chance because we're so focused on the process of being productive.

Compared to fifty years ago, we have better tools available to us. Computers and technology have allowed us to do more in less time. We have easy and virtually unlimited access to information, which has allowed us to grow and expand our thinking. And yet, all we have done with that is to obsess more and more on systemization and process-building to increase efficiency and productivity.

There is something critical missing: "people" got taken out of the equation with the advent of mass production, when organizational metaphors became machine-based.

Before mass production, business focused on individual craftsmen who produced goods from start to finish. Even though workers didn't necessarily depend on each other to complete their work, business—and society as a whole—was built on the relationship between those craftsmen. The mindset was one of commonwealth and collaboration driven by a network of relationships. It was a far more 'organic' way of operating.

With mass production came a change to the way we saw society. Organizations structured themselves as machines: a collection of parts with very specific functions and very little discretion or room for initiative. And so the industrial mindset was born: as long as every part of the machine does what it is supposed to do, we can drive the machine and be productive. If a part tries to do 'its own thing' or questions the design, productivity will fall. The solution? Do everything possible to prevent that happening by enforcing secrecy, carefully controlled messages, and strict hierarchy.

We need to go back to a more organic way of running businesses, with a focus on relationships and being able to respond to the needs of individuals.

Why do organizations focus so much on process over people?

The reason organizations would rather focus on process than people is simple: it's easier and faster. You can use logic to plan and describe a process. You can standardize it. You can create risk mitigation plans around it. And you get to feel good if you've hit your numbers, so you feel productive.

What it creates are toxic *employee* experiences that create toxic *customer* experiences.

Let's take Wells Fargo for example. At the end of 2016, the bank was dragged into the glare of negative publicity because its agents had been mis-selling products just to meet quotas. Six months later, several major Canadian banks fell foul of regulators for similar reasons. In both cases, employees spoke openly about being in fear of their jobs if they didn't hit their targets. They knew it didn't feel right, but the process forced them to do it.

Now, is it likely that those banks intended to sell inappropriate products to their customers?

No. So, the process is out of line with the organization's purpose and identity and values, and it's forcing people to do things that are out of line with their purpose and identity and values. Figure 11. Welcome to full dysfunction.

It happens in all sorts of organizations, and not only in sales.

When a production manager is under increasing pressure to squeeze every second of productive time out of machinery, and the orders are piling up, it's tempting to space out inspections. It's tempting to loosen some of the inspection criteria. The result? Quality issues. Returns. Shortened product life. All the problems that consumers increasingly complain about, even for companies that have traditionally prided themselves on their product quality.

In service industries, how many organizations actually reward employees for engaging in deep conversation with a customer? How many reward front-line staff for their contribution to customer loyalty? Loyalty is something that's hard to measure, and even harder to attribute. How does one interaction build loyalty? It doesn't: it's a series of interactions, and they may each involve different people on different teams. That's another reason why it's so important to think of the organization as a network of teams.

Companies like Southwest Airlines and Ritz-Carlton operate this way. Every Ritz-Carlton employee has $2,000 discretion every day to fix the guests' experience or delight them, and everyone is responsible for the customer experience.

It's ironic that the way to bring our organizations kicking and screaming into the 21st century is to return to values that worked in the 18th century, but it's no more outrageous than running a modern IT company or bank with a model that developed in the age of cotton mills and steam engines.

We have advanced so far with technology, and the new ways of working that those technologies allow have created spectacular increases in efficiency and productivity, and yet our ways of *managing* haven't kept pace.

And it's not that we have to put ourselves back to the dark ages. It's simply that the pre-mechanistic way of doing business relied heavily on relationships, as I said, but also on people's individual skills, their results and ability to get the job done. That is what we need to reintegrate into business.

The mechanistic way of managing—the industrial mindset—is built on a false illusion of control. With a (real) machine, there is a level of certainty: you know that if you give the machine certain inputs, in the right proportions, and run it for a defined period of time, you'll get a predictable output done to a predictable quality standard. Human machines don't work like that because humans aren't machines. Humans are too unpredictable, and human markets too unstable.

And so, we have become overly focused on process and compliance. The crazier VUCA gets, the more we are trying to hold on to predictability and stability. We strive to protect ourselves against risk and ensure the "right" parties are being held accountable.

At the same time, organizations are being held to higher standards than they used to be. In the nineteenth century, and for much of the twentieth, organizations were answerable to virtually no one but their shareholders. Now they have to satisfy the needs of many disparate *stake*holders: employees, communities, interest groups, government, regulators, society as a whole, and many others besides.

The interaction of those three factors—VUCA, litigiousness, and the number of stakeholders—adds up to an increase in complexity for the organization and its leaders.

In the process, however, they've lost sight of the impact on the individual. Because now you have human beings caught between the volatility of the real world and the inflexibility of the constructed process, and there's only one thing that can give: the human beings who are supposed to be implementing the process.

> Hiring and firing are two very tightly defined processes in most organizations.
>
> On one occasion, a position opened up on my team. There were two candidates: Suzy, who was already a member of my team but in a different capacity, and Jane, who wanted to join my team. Jane was highly qualified for the role, despite being the outsider, and Suzy thought she was perfect for the role but really wasn't.
>
> Naturally, I chose Jane and, in accordance with the hiring process, I got the team together—including Jane and Suzy, of course—and announced my decision.
>
> It would have been very easy for me to take meet Suzy before the meeting and say, "Suzy, thank you for applying. I'm really glad you wanted to be in this role. We

> do have another candidate, and I'm giving her the position for these reasons...." Instead, I was so focused on following the process that HR had laid out that I didn't think about the impact I was having.
>
> My relationship with Suzy after that point was never quite the same. At times it became quite confrontational, and we ended up having a very frank discussion in which she finally opened up and said, "I felt horrible when you did that. It was like you just set me up in front of the whole team."

When the pace of life was slower, that could be managed. It was easier to keep the pyramids aligned, and the winds of VUCA were weaker and less frequent. So, a good leader could see a problem developing and intervene. They could change the process and respond to the new environment.

How does Purposeful Workplace Experience™ help?

"Connect to People Not Process" means that, as a leader, you start from the organization's purpose, identity, and beliefs and values, and you look beyond process to connect and align with the individual; you have to address the whole bottom triangle (Figure 14).

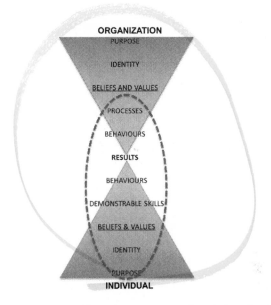

Figure 14: Look beyond Process to connect to the whole individual

You have a decision to make. You can either get bogged down in the processes and metrics, which is where the logical part of your brain wants to go, or you can address that other triangle: "How do these values and beliefs now relate to the beliefs and values of the individuals within my organization? Is there a good fit?"

You already put controls in place to manage financial performance. That is about managing the tip of both pyramids: results. HR processes usually focus on the upper part of the employee triangle—the part in front of the Trust Boundary. They focus on skills and behaviours. The Purposeful Workplace Experience™ is about looking at what's beyond the Trust Boundary on both triangles.

That was what created the shears that allowed the misalignments we saw in earlier chapters to appear (see Figure 8, Figure 10, and Figure 11): it was easier to line up and adjust those 'visible' parts of the pyramids than to try to realign the whole pyramid. That is how we created Enron and other similar situations.

The greater the level of alignment you can create, the more productive your workforce will be, and that will feed down directly to the bottom line. That is the big benefit of creating a Purposeful Workplace Experience™.

Authenticity and leadership

Where does connection start? With authenticity. Leaders need to be authentic. They need to admit who they really are instead of trying to project an ideal image. They need to let go of the need to try to keep everything under control.

But what do we really mean when we say "authentic"?

Authenticity is the process of moving the Trust Boundary and bringing more of who we are to work. Now, for most people, the thought of revealing their true identity and purpose and discussing values and beliefs at work is terrifying.

Think about why that is the case. You have no idea what the reaction will be, so you're opening yourself up to the unpredictable. And you open yourself up to the risk that someone will say "you don't belong here," putting all three Base Needs in jeopardy.

The advantage of this is that by revealing more of ourselves at work, we engender trust. It's much easier for two people to trust each other when there is less hidden away below the waterline—and that applies between two work colleagues, between a leader and a follower, and between a company and an employee.

VUCA has driven this need to be vulnerable and authentic. Life moves too fast these days for things to be anything but real and vulnerable, it's impossible for any one person to stay caught up and informed on everything, and you have to be prepared to admit that you don't know everything.

Moving away from hierarchy doesn't mean you don't have performance management systems. You need to have oversight around what employees are doing. But, when you have more touchpoints, and you take the time to connect with more people, you build trust—in both directions. And trust is the foundation of any team. There are always going to be differences of opinion but, when there is trust within the team, people are happy to express their concerns and bring them to their manager, because they are not worried that's it's going to damage their relationship. That creates a much more open work environment.

So, the first rule of engagement is *Connect to People, not Process*. Many leaders think that they have been doing that. They have lavished every single employee with individual attention, managed their performance, and held them personally accountable. But the focus of that management was only for the tip of the triangle: on behaviours and results. The focus was not on the individual, but on individual performance. It didn't recognize all the effort—individual and collective— that was needed to create those results. It ignored the impact of circumstances on performance, which can often hide or distort individual capability.

We need to focus on *people*, not *the person*. That means we need to encourage relationships, so we have to have trust.

That, in turn, means people have to understand each other's values and beliefs and purpose, and the only way to build trust is by opening up the trust box: by showing what's in the lower levels of their triangles.

How to start focusing on people

"Focusing on people" starts with recognizing the bottom of the individual triangle. This is nothing new: many great leaders do this already. The astonishing thing, however, is how many leaders *aren't* doing this. They are stuck at the bottom of Maslow's hierarchy managing, controlling, and dictating.

When you are with someone, be *with* them: put down your smartphone and turn away from your computer screen.

Take a few minutes each day to have a conversation, and remember that, however "democratic" your outlook, you are automatically placed on a podium because of hierarchical positioning. You make decisions that impact people, so the natural inclination is to please you, or at least not *dis*please you, until they know how you will react.

Remember, too, that we all like predictability. You can connect with people if your actions and responses have a tone of predictability. That doesn't mean that your responses themselves—the words you use—need to be predictable, but rather the tone of the response.

In *The Speed of Trust*[25], Steven M R Covey describes 'trust' as being like a bank account: you have to put into it to take out. Connecting with someone puts coins in your trust bank with that person. As Covey points out, the coins that one person might value don't necessarily have any value for the other, so you need to think about what will build trust in the other person: you may not see the value in a few minutes of authentic conversation with a team member, but to them it may mean the world.

What does connection look like? Ask and listen, rather than telling. Hold people accountable, but show that you will be too, and give people examples of what that will look like.

One critical aspect of connection is to let people know that it's OK to make mistakes. You can do that by sharing examples of times when you made a mistake. It doesn't have to be a huge mistake that cost a million dollars, but when people know you are human, they know it is OK for them to be human too.

As Patrick Lencioni[26] points out, the foundation of teamwork is trust, and that requires you to *"overcome [your] need for invulnerability."* In a high-functioning team, people aren't afraid to be honest, they are *"unafraid to air their dirty laundry, admit their mistakes, their weaknesses and concerns without fear of reprisal."*

I'm not saying you have to give people *carte blanche* to screw up. It's simply the recognition that mistakes will happen.

---

[25] The SPEED of Trust: The One Thing That Changes Everything. Feb 5 2008 by Stephen M.R. Covey and Stephen R. Covey
[26] The Five Dysfunctions of a Team: A Leadership Fable   Apr 11 2002 by Patrick Lencioni

And yes, there are times when you simply can't afford a mistake, but there are also times when it's OK. You have to help your team to know when they absolutely can't afford to make a mistake, and when they can.

> *"It is not the critic who counts; not the man who points out how the strong man stumbles, or where the doer of deeds could have done them better. The credit belongs to the man who is actually in the arena, whose face is marred by dust and sweat and blood; who strives valiantly; . . . who at the best knows, in the end, the triumph of high achievement, and who at worst, if he fails, at least fails while daring greatly."*
> —**Theodore Roosevelt**

There's no rulebook, and there never will be

You can't prepare for every possible situation, which means you can't create all the possible solutions. We didn't have enough rules before when we were trying to deflect accountability, and yet now we want rules to define everything and leave no room for interpretation. It's as though when we saw the rules we had weren't working, we decided we just didn't have enough rules.

That is simply not possible: there is never going to be a rulebook because you can't cover every single rule.

It's like trying to write down the psychological contract and embody it in the employment contract. It can't be done.

There are always going to be situations that emerge, and you have to recognize that and deal with them as they arise.

In some senses, that's why the psychological contract broke in the first place: we tried to overregulate.

The Wells Fargo mis-selling scandal gives us a wonderful example of this. Wells Fargo had values—they were laid out in their glossy brochures and on the corporate website. And values give you goalposts. But leaders need to help people to understand how to apply those values. Model the values yourself. Give your team members examples of the values applied in everyday situations. Rather than asking for a yes/no answer to everything, ask them to show how the values led them to make the decision they did. That is all part of connecting.

> ## WATCH THE VIDEOS
>
> Want to learn more about the
> Purposeful Workplace Experience?
>
> Visit this site to watch me speak about it.
>
> **http://pinnacleculture.ca/bookvideos/**

Summary

❖ Organizations have hyper-focused on process to drive efficiency. Now it's time to focus on people first.

❖ Starting with people means understanding what is at the bottom of their triangle, below the waterline.

❖ Connection starts with authenticity. This means moving the trust boundary and strengthening relationships.

❖ This is done through conversations which builds trust. Then your behaviour becomes predictable, even when the situation you're facing isn't.

Chapter Ten

The Rule of Collaboration: "Create opportunities to collaborate, and minimize competition"

VUCA happens so fast and so hard that one person cannot manage it alone. You need to leverage the strengths of as many people as possible because even when you do make a decision, you're still not going to be 100% confident that it's the *right* decision.

It's far easier—and far more likely—for people to respond to a decision and act on it in an authentic way if they have been involved in the decision-making process. When people are involved with creating a plan, it's much easier for them to engage with it and take ownership of it. That is one of your strongest lines of defence when VUCA hits.

There's also great power in diversity. And I don't mean demographic diversity: I mean idea diversity; getting the different viewpoints and opinions, which usually means you end up with diversity of options.

Now, that might sound like a recipe for chaos and indecisiveness, and in a non-Purposeful Workplace Experience™

workplace, it would be. The difference Purposeful Workplace Experience™ makes to group decision-making is that the decisions are values-based. As long as everyone's values are aligned, then the options you create are likely to share common purpose and intent, and to be acceptable to the majority of the group. That creates a strong anchor in times of uncertainty: you know that the plan you are following was based on positive principles and will keep things moving in the right direction. It's not just a knee-jerk reaction.

In the absence of that—when people aren't anchored in values, and they don't know why decisions are made—when the going gets tough, they will probably wobble, or at least feel uncertain and unconfident.

Without the values-based background that you get in a Purposeful Workplace Experience™, you have a group of people who are acting in response to a situation but with no vision or grounding. The result just adds to the unpredictability of any situation, and responses might not be consistent. Values create consistency.

When things are unpredictable and unstable, the confidence that you are doing the right thing is eroded if you don't know what "the right thing" is. There is not a single leader who believes it's easy to make the right decision when the situation is highly ambiguous. So, when you have this collaboration, it gives increased confidence to everybody, which leads to stronger commitment.

Collaboration, when it is anchored in values, helps people to bring their own personal values into a decision, and it can help members of the team who may be feeling disconnected from the team and corporate values to bring themselves into alignment. It does that because the act of collaboration—

when that collaboration is open and honest, and not grounded in fear—encourages those collaborating to share and participate.

The Danger of Group-Think

The only time when collaboration fails is when it is replaced by group-think. Group-think can happen when you have a collection of people who haven't connected to their values, and whose thoughts are dominated by the fear of losing their Base Needs.

It can also happen when a group doesn't engage in healthy conflict, like debating the pros and cons of a proposal or deliberately poking holes in arguments.

So, true collaboration requires a group of people with different viewpoints. They may be drawn from different divisions, or simply represent different perspectives and personalities. The key is that they have to have the confidence and freedom to be authentic. It's that safe environment that is critical; that is what stops the group-think.

And that safe-environment requires connection: someone can't feel safe if they're talking to someone they feel no connection to.

Why collaboration is difficult

In too many organizations, collaboration is hard to achieve simply because corporate reward and promotion structures don't support it. In fact, many performance management systems drive the exact opposite behaviour: there is a big disconnect between what the organization says they value and what their reward systems do value. And what many rewards systems value is individual achievement.

Workplaces are set up to encourage competition through performance ratings and job promotions. People compare their rating as though it was an objective measure. On one occasion, one of my direct reports came up to me. She found out the rating another team member had received, and she disagreed with it. I said, "Do you know what was on his personal development plan?" "No." "Then how can you judge his rating?"

Walk into a sales workshop anywhere in the world, and you will see a mindset of "healthy competition" at work. I used to think this fuelled performance. And it does. But it is short-term, and it comes with a cost. These training workshops are full of mini-rewards for performance. For example, the team that comes first gets to eat at the buffet first. Small competitive incentives like this seem harmless. However, they foster an "us" versus "them" mentality. When a team isn't winning, it can also create feelings of fear and guilt: "What happens if we lose?" "I'll be letting my boss down if our group doesn't win this competition."

You might get good performance for the next few months, but it's not sustainable over time. It doesn't create an atmosphere or climate that encourages people to work together. It simply creates an imperative to out-do each other.

With competition, there is always a winner and loser. Leaders need to go out of their way to give people permission to collaborate and proactively mitigate feelings of fear and guilt.

I'm not saying competition is bad. I'm not encouraging a mindless "Everyone must get prizes" approach. I'm simply saying that we need to focus our competitive urges on beating the competition rather than our colleagues!

Because of the way promotions and even employee retention policies are set, most performance appraisals are a zero-sum game. In order for one employee to score highly, someone else has to be pushed down the rankings. Many companies are moving away from blindly applying a bell curve, but too many still tell a manager to reward the top twenty percent of their performers and fire the bottom ten percent, even if they'd be the top performer in another team.

So, if it's a zero-sum game, then competition becomes unhealthy, and you pay a heavy opportunity cost in reduced creativity and innovation.

Reward people for stretching their comfort zone

In a zero-sum, up-or-out environment, people are often afraid to take risks. After all, if one misstep could cost you your job or at least lose you a bonus, there's no incentive to do anything unless you know it will succeed.

In a world of VUCA, that's a recipe for disaster. The point is, the things that have always worked usually stop working when VUCA hits. You have to innovate your way out of VUCA, rather than doubling down on strategies that are already starting to fall apart.

That's impossible to do if people aren't used to innovating and taking a chance. So, you need to give permission to direct reports and colleagues to take risks and move out of their comfort zone.

Senior leaders and managers have to be willing to be vulnerable and to share the mistakes they have made, the impact it had and what they learned from it.

How to promote collaboration over competition

How do we, practically, switch to a culture where collaboration is valued over internal competition?

As a leader, you can make a difference, and you can build a collective voice.

We have to face the fact that you can't change the whole organization. But if you start by changing what you can—your team—word will spread, and other managers will learn from your experience.

Being the first manager to try this can feel lonely and vulnerable. In his TED talk *How to Start a Movement*[27], Derek Sivers shares a video that illustrates the importance of two people: the first person to do something and the second—what he calls the *first follower*.

In the video, a group of people is sitting on a hillside, and someone has a boombox playing loudly. One person gets up and starts to dance wildly. As you might expect, everyone stares at him a little oddly. That goes on for a little time, with most people trying to ignore him until a complete stranger walks up and joins him. Within moments someone else joins

---

[27] http://bit.ly/TEDmovement

in, then another, then a few more. Suddenly people are rushing to get up and join in, and before you know it, the whole hillside is dancing.

Until the follower joins in, it's just a lone nut dancing. It's the follower that turns the nut into a leader. So, do what you think is right, and others will follow.

Are You a Super Chicken?

> "Ellen, I don't want to be a super chicken! I've been trying to be a super chicken for most of my career, and I'm sick of it."
>
> Of course, my poor friend Ellen had no idea what I was talking about, but what I was saying was that I'd had an epiphany.

In many organizations, top performers and employees identified as future top performers are often streamed into some form of 'high potential' program, designed to encourage them and advance them by presenting them with opportunities they would not, otherwise, be offered.

On the surface, that's a perfectly reasonable idea, and it is one that we are trained to expect and accept right from school. That doesn't make it a good idea, however.

In a highly entertaining TED talk[28], renowned author, documentary producer, and CEO Margaret Heffernan discusses the results of an experiment to breed 'super chickens' that

---

[28] http://bit.ly/TEDchicken

would be more productive than 'standard' chickens (measured by the number of eggs laid).

The breeder put all the average egg-layers together in one group, and the "top-performing" egg-layers into a second group. He repeated this process on six successive generations.

So, what do you think happened by the time six generations had been streamed?

Most people would expect that the top-performer group was producing more eggs. What happened, instead, was that the average group was doing very well: they were plump and fully feathered, and egg production had increased. The second group—the "high potential" program—had resulted in carnage: they had pecked each other to death, and only three were still alive by the end of the study. The highly-productive chickens, who—remember—had been laying their eggs happily while they were in the general environment, spent more time on pecking each other than on their productivity once they were segregated.

Now, we may not be managing chickens, but we've all seen employees in an 'up or out' management environment indulge in self-promoting behaviours at the expense of other team members. You have probably done it yourself and been rewarded. And we've all seen teams indulge in self-promoting behaviours at the expense of other teams. When you have a high-performing team, and you have to rank them, you are knocking down people who are really high performers; people who on any other team would be a star. And they do whatever it takes to stay at the top of the group—even if it isn't in the best interest of anyone but themselves. All of those behaviours happen at the expense of the organization—and yet organizations continue to encourage it!

Becoming collaborative

So, if you've decided to get out of the business of breeding super chickens, how do you move towards a more collaborative culture?

First, we need to let go of the economic belief that having a group of people maximizing their individual self-interest will ultimately maximize the collective interest.

I call this notion that we look after ourselves first and foremost the "economic" belief because it is primarily promoted by economists. When an economist visits the supermarket, all he sees is a crowd of would-be shoplifters kept in check only by a quick mental comparison of the cost of lost status and freedom if they are caught, to the economic benefit of not paying for a bag of Cheetos. Their view of the workplace is equally gloomy: all that keeps stationery in the stationery cupboard is that people are afraid they will be caught and fired.

That's a very cynical view of human nature, but it drives the competitive model of management. And it just isn't true. As Maslow and Lieberman both tell us, humans are wired to work together, and we want to belong to a group. It is nonsense to think that people just act out of selfish and isolated self-interest.

Think about yourself. Do you help your colleagues? If you do, what motivates you to do it? Is it because you get rewarded for it? If the economic belief were true, you would only help colleagues if there was a direct benefit to you. If the economic belief were true, you would need a clause in your contract that gave you a point, or a bonus, or some other reward every time you did something nice for someone else. The truth is, you do it because it is the right thing to do. What gets in the way of collaboration are internal structures and our mindset.

Where to start

The first place you can start is in meetings. Most agendas are overly ambitious. Typically, people fill their agendas with far more things than can be accomplished in a short period of time. So, build time into your agendas for people to digest and process and discuss.

Set a clear objective to keep everyone focused, and then encourage new ideas and share information as much as possible—oversharing is only a problem when people choose to share the wrong things.

Another way to engage is to actively solicit ideas and to ask questions rather than directing, even if you know the answer: you probably know, or at least have a very good idea of, the direction things will take. Recognize that, while you know that, the journey is not about you getting the answer first: it is about bringing everybody along together. So, give them time to synthesize and process to get there with you. Learn how to ask deeper questions, open-ended and thought-provoking. Aim to make people think, not just do.

Remember that all of this has to be authentic. If you ask people to collaborate, be prepared to recognize the value created by collaboration. If you ask for input, be prepared to use it.

And if you ask for feedback, be prepared to take it and act on it.

As a leader, it is important you are at the front, driving the vehicle and setting the direction. However, you are not necessarily going to be the one planning the route: what you are saying, in effect, is "We are at A, and we need to get to Z. There are a lot of ways we could get there, so let's figure out, collectively, the best path to take."

Interestingly, the leaders who foster collaboration most successfully will often actively encourage conflict and disagreement. They go out of their way to make sure they look at things from all angles and give their followers permission to disagree and even to play devil's advocate.

We rely heavily on words when we collaborate, mistakenly believing everyone sees the situation the same way we do.

One of the best ways to get everyone onto the same page is— quite literally—with a page. Pick up a pen and draw whatever you're talking about. It doesn't have to be a work of art: use lines, circles, stick people. The key is to use visuals to draw out the situation.

One of my former bosses, a VP was a real master at this. When she asked people to contribute, her body language matched: she would lean in, make eye contact, and really listen to what you had to say. And you knew she was listening, because she would ask probing questions; she would get you to elaborate when your logic wasn't clear; she would highlight where the two of you were—or weren't—aligned in your thinking; and she would connect your ideas back to what had already been said.

Her agendas always allowed time for dialogue and, at the end, she would distill the conversation down to a visual representation. It was incredibly powerful because it simplified what everyone had said and highlighted potential gaps in understanding or differences in interpretation. There is great power in jumping up and drawing a quick visual on a whiteboard or flipchart and just drawing a quick visual to represent what everyone is agreeing to.

Finally, great leaders reinforce collaboration by acknowledging contributions to the process. It's not just about the deliverable: it is also about how the group got to it, and the role each person played in that journey. That means naming names and calling out specific examples.

Many leaders hesitate to encourage collaboration because it can feel slower than having a single individual driving ahead. It can even feel, at times, like you're going around in circles.

It can also feel like collaboration is being forced. There are times when collaboration isn't needed, particularly in decision-making. Is it a process decision with little risk? Then you probably don't need to collaborate. Is the scope broad? Is the situation complex? Is there a greater degree of risk? Will the impact reach beyond your span of control? Then it can be useful to get more diverse viewpoints in order to fully assess what is going on.

There is no sense in collaborating if your team doesn't have trust and you don't have healthy conflict. That's where a lot of time gets wasted.

If you find yourself feeling frustrated about a collaborative decision, then you are focusing on your individual need to get the job done and move on to the next task, rather than focusing on the journey the group has to take. Ultimately, the purpose of collaboration is to create something together, not to check items off your to-do list. The path may take longer, but the decision is likely to be better, and the outcome more beneficial. A single decision-maker, working alone, can find themselves struggling for ideas, disappearing down blind alleys, and not always getting the job done or getting there more slowly.

In my Director role, I realized that the success of our team relied on how well I collaborated with two other Directors, since there were many interdependencies of our groups.

The company was heading into an exciting period of several product launches, and there were a lot of regulatory approvals required. However, all three of us were new to our teams, and we had inherited an environment in which all three teams worked in silos, which wasn't very effective. If we were to have any chance to get the products to market in a timely fashion, we had to come together and create a process that would allow our departments—about thirty people in all—to work together.

In the end, we managed to bring all thirty people into alignment in less than six months. We did it by working collaboratively—not just the leaders, but also the members of all three teams—which in turn required us to be totally open. We knew where A was, and where Z was, but we abandoned all our preconceptions about how we got there, and we were open to any and all ideas.

We turned discussions into visual representations on whiteboards. We also created process maps together and took the diagrams and the process maps back to

> our teams. To reinforce the focus on collaborative working, we called out anyone who demonstrated behaviours that took things in the right direction and got people out of their silos.

There was a lot of trust between the three of us. We were very comfortable pushing each other and engaging in "healthy" conflict, and we were willing to try things that might fail and admit when we were wrong.

In the end, we were successful in streamlining the process, and all the products got market approval. We cut down on the level of frustration and reduced the work required to create submissions to the regulators, and the quality of our submissions went up.

WATCH THE VIDEOS

Want to learn more about the Purposeful Workplace Experience?

Visit this site to watch me speak about it.

http://pinnacleculture.ca/bookvideos/

Summary

❖ Collaboration encourages diverse thinking and when it is based around shared values leads to individuals feeling confident and safe to contribute.

❖ Be aware of group-think as this can be unhealthy for a team. It can occur if trust isn't high between team members and stifles sharing of opinions.

❖ Competition is embedded into many workplaces and can drive short-term results. However, it can also stifle individual contribution as one might be afraid to be wrong and "lose".

❖ Top performers drive individual results but also need to contribute to high-performing teams in a collaborative, not competitive, manner.

❖ Creating a more collaborative environment can start with meetings: minimize agenda items, create time to discuss issues instead of just giving updates; encourage differing thought and stimulate healthy conflict; use a whiteboard to draw out and visualize what is being said.

Chapter Eleven

The Rule of Adaptability: "Be adaptable and expect your plans to change"

When you live in a world of VUCA, you can't afford to be rigid and stick to the program. You have to be willing to flex and adapt.

When Paul and I got married, we had a strategic life plan in place. Children were central to that plan. I was an only child so, at least initially, I wanted five, although that was blissful ignorance.

Just after we conceived our first son, however, Paul was diagnosed and VUCA hit us hard. Even with that diagnosis, we stuck to the plan, and so after our first son, we had the second. In many respects, it was our way of saying to the Universe, "We are still going to do what we planned."

Initially, we also had other plans: I was going to be a VP of HR and Paul wanted to open a motorcycle shop. We were going to grow old together.

When VUCA hit, we had to change our plans. We still had children, but only two, and we only got seven years of marriage—six of them dominated by cancer.

Paul's illness also forced us into a quarterly planning cycle: we lived from CT scan to CT scan, which just happened to be three months apart, and each quarter we had to reassess where we were and recalibrate the tactics for the next period.

For some quarters, Paul would be getting Chemo, which meant we had to go to the hospital every week and he would be sick afterward. We had to make big adjustments to accommodate that, and I had to move my work schedule around.

Sometimes the CT scan would lead to a change in treatment. One time, he was prescribed pills, which gave us more flexibility.

I took that mindset of living from CT scan to CT scan and adjusting our plans back into the workplace: we still had our strategy—whether it was the business strategy or a personal development plan—but we expected to alter it every quarter to meet the changing business conditions.

In recent years, market-leading companies that once seemed unassailable have been wiped from our memories by the unexpected. Blockbuster, once a common sight on every main street across North America and the United Kingdom, is now just a cautionary tale in a range of business books discussing what happens when you fail to adapt to market shifts.

This chapter is about saving your company from becoming a cautionary tale.

With VUCA, the world—and your markets—are constantly changing. The only way to deal with that is to allow people to deviate from plans, to be flexible with your planning, and allow yourself to respond as an organization.

You can't afford to be rigid and to follow the program blindly: you have to be willing to flex and adapt. Indeed, it's a case of adapt or die.

"Greater organizational agility leads to better performance—providing organizations with a powerful edge on the competition."[29]

In Primed to Perform[30], Neel Doshi and Lindsay McGregor introduced the idea of *adaptive performance*: the ability to deviate from a tactical plan.

That's a useful distinction because we are not talking about abandoning the overall strategy anytime something changes in our environment. We are simply advocating that you focus on the strategy, rather than obsess on the tactics. It's not about suddenly going in a different direction: you still move in the same direction, but accept that there are other routes you could take to get to the same endpoint.

Tactical plans are necessary, but you have to know when to deviate from it. When things go wrong, it can be fatal to simply dig in your heels and insist, "This is the plan, and we have to go with it." Usually what ends up happening in that situation is that, while you are defending a plan that is clearly

---

[29] PMI, Organizational Agility Report, 2012
[30] Primed to Perform: How to Build the Highest Performing Cultures Through the Science of Total Motivation, 2015 - by Neel Doshi and Lindsay McGregor

not going to work, your customer base is thinking, "What the ****? Why didn't you respond to this media statement?" When your tablet computers start to blow up, you have to stop the production line and think about a redesign. You can't just say, "The plan says we have to produce 20,000 units today. We can't stop the line."

So, you have to know when to stick to the plan, but also when to deviate. You also have to recognize that you *will* deviate, and knowing that, you prepare: What are you going to think about when you deviate? What questions are you going to ask yourself?

This is an important concept to introduce to your team and to your organization. When I introduced it to my team, my first step was to tell them, "Here's our plan, but we need to acknowledge that we are going to have to deviate."

The reaction was predictable: "But, what do you mean?"

I replied, "Well, something's going to happen, so let's just acknowledge, first of all, the fact that something will happen that will cause us to shift gears."

Scenario Planning helps, but it doesn't go far enough

You may have come across the idea of scenario planning: creating variations of a plan that anticipate a variety of possible future situations.

Scenario planning is a good way to start cultivating adaptability, since it explicitly recognizes that the future may not go the way we need it to. But it doesn't get us all the way to full adaptability. It still doesn't recognize the unpredictable. It doesn't account for a situation where you are completely blindsided: and that is what VUCA does.

You can think about the difference between scenario planning and full adaptability like this.

Scenario planning focuses on the *content* of a situation. It's about responding directly to what is happening. In other words, it is primarily tactical. "We want to get from A to Z, but if this happens we will head to S instead, and if this happens, we will head for M."

Adaptability focuses on the *context* of the situation: it is about managing the overall strategy. "We still want to get to Z, but we may have to rethink how we get there, and it may take us longer."

One of the biggest problems with scenario planning is simply that many organizations do it badly. They create a series of scenarios and then treat it like a beauty parade: "Which of these would be best for us?" The problem is, you don't get to choose which scenario is going to play out. The world does that, and it can easily ignore your scenarios completely and throw something unexpected at you. That means that, even with scenario planning, you can still be blindsided. But it can be worse because then you're trying to shoehorn one of your preplanned scenarios into the situation.

So, scenario planning has some merits, because if you are considering a range of different scenarios from various viewpoints, you are going to be less tied to The Plan.

It's about managing reality

You need to know how to get from A to Z and bear in mind that there are many different ways you can get there. Don't be too attached to one way or the other.

Now, one of the big challenges when it comes to being adaptable is that it flies in the face of people's need for certainty. There is comfort in having a plan and knowing that, as long as you do what the plan demands, you will be OK. When someone says, "You need to know when to deviate from the plan," it takes away all the certainty you had.

The conflict between Adaptability and Planning

Being adaptable doesn't require you to throw away your tactical plan. You need to plan properly to have a successful business. Having a plan gives you focus, it tells you where you are going—and it's important to know where you are going—and it allows you to track your progress.

There is an inherent conflict between adaptability and planning, because planning is about creating certainty and predictability, whereas adaptability is about recognizing uncertainty and unpredictability. The purpose of adaptability is to make you more responsive and ready to address whatever happens head on.

And therein lies the conflict. Most of the time, the plan becomes a contract. You agree to your annual plan, and that's it for the rest of the year: you are beaten over the head with it constantly. "Are you on-plan? Why are you not on-plan? What are your variances from it?"

Lead and Lagging Indicators

A critical concept to understand is the distinction between a lead indicator and a lagging indicator.

A lead indicator is something that tells you *what is likely to happen*. In *If It's Raining in Brazil, Buy Starbucks*, Peter Navarro points out the connection between tropical weather patterns and the price of coffee. So, rainfall in Brazil is a lead indicator of coffee prices.

A lagging indicator is something that tells you *what already happened*. Revenue and profit are both lagging indicators. They tell you about the sales you made and the expenses you paid last month, last quarter, last year or whenever.

Most organizations are much better at identifying lagging indicators than lead indicators, and we need to get better at spotting those lead indicators. It is the lead indicators that can help us to spot VUCA before it hits us, and can help us embrace adaptability more easily.

Shorter Planning Cycles Help

It's easier to be adaptable if you're not locked into long planning cycles. Most organizations are still hostage to the annual plan. Knowing that your business plan will probably change, however, it makes sense to reduce the time and effort invested in the planning cycle. So, you need to find ways to shorten the planning process, and you can reallocate that time to future iterations. So, the net amount of time spent planning remains broadly similar, but it is spread out across the year.

In my own team, we switched to quarterly plans. Every three months, we would look at what was going on and reassess: "Are things going the way we thought they were? What uncertainty is there in the market? Where do we think something is going to come out of left field?"

Now, you may be thinking, *But we only just manage to find the time and resources to do planning once a year, and it disrupts our work for weeks—even months. How am I supposed to plan on a quarterly basis when it takes longer than that to prepare the plan in the first place?*

The point is, I'm not suggesting you need to replan and set a new direction every three months. Think of it like navigating your car.

In the old days, before dashboard GPS and smartphones, you would contact your drivers association—in Canada, it was the CAA—a month ahead, and they would print out a big map and a list of dozens or hundreds of turn-by-turn instructions which they mailed to you printed out on a stack of paper. Sometimes it was out of date even before you set off because there might be a construction or a road closure along the route.

When you set off on your journey, you'd take the printout with you in the car, and you just had to hope there were no accidents, jams or diversions *en route*, because if there were, you had no way of updating the directions, and if you strayed from the planned route or missed a turn, you would get lost, and it might take you hours to find your way back.

Compare that to how we plan routes today. We program our destination into our phone, and it works out an optimized route. As we drive, it constantly tracks where we are and what is going on around us. It warns us about any problems coming up, and it automatically calculates a detour to get around those problems. It's still taking you to the same place, it's just that you may take longer to get there.

Annual planning is rather like that old stack of printouts. You know where you wanted to go when you started, and how you expected to get there. When conditions change, it very quickly gets out of date, but you don't know what else to do, so you try to stick to it.

When you shorten the planning cycle, you're able to track progress and continuously monitor where you are. You can adjust to conditions and adjust your approach to suit.

The long and winding road to nowhere

The truly sad thing about those over-extended planning cycles is that usually when a company has to put so much time and effort into planning, they are no more accurate than if they made a quick estimate.

The further you are looking into the future, the more you are having to guess what is likely to happen, and the more dubious your assumptions become. So you dedicate more resources than necessary to generate those assumptions, and then you and your boss, or a central planning team, spend unnecessary hours arguing over the accuracy of your assumptions, and massaging them to fit around a separate set of assumptions coming down from above. And both sides forget that they are basically arguing over whose horoscope is more accurate!

Annual planning, in effect, pushes the risk into quarter two onwards. Why? Because most managers approach the exercise from the point of view that they know what's going to happen for the next three months, and so they plan those and then create a worst-case scenario for the other quarters. Which begs the question: why bother planning the other quarters?

If everyone spent less time making assumptions about what might happen twelve months out, you could come back in three months and make a more meaningful adjustment then.

It's Not Just About the Budget

It would be easy to assume that I'm talking solely about the financial plan and budget. But, what I'm saying applies to all the planning that takes place in an organization, including employee performance planning.

Take personal development and career planning, for example. When I was a manager, we would plan our personal objectives for the year, and we would make them SMART (specific, measurable, aligned, realistic and time-bound). January to March would be spot on because that was the first quarter. Anything beyond that, however, was like throwing spaghetti at the wall: it was almost impossible to accurately predict the timing or extent of our successes.

> One member of my team, in particular, was disadvantaged by the annual cycle and had been deemed an underperformer.

Part of the problem was that the environment in which this person worked was extremely volatile and unpredictable, and people didn't really understand that area.

Switching to quarterly performance discussions allowed us to be much clearer with the objectives because we had a better line of sight, which set them up to get a better rating.

Of course, it wasn't just about getting a better rating for my direct report. It had to translate into better performance, as well.

In this specific case, because we were able to be clearer on expectations, both within and outside the team, we were able to show a direct improvement in the employee's delivery against those expectations.

The Hidden Blocks to Adaptability

According to Deloitte's 2017 Global Human Capital Report, agility and collaboration are critical to organizational success: 94% of companies recognize the importance of those skills, and yet 70% of CEOs say that their organization lacks the skills needed to adapt.

In Primed to Perform, Doshi and McGregor discuss how to help your organization be more adaptable. They identify six motivators which drive human performance and help people to adapt. Three of them are what they call *direct* motivators, and three are *indirect*.

Let's look specifically at one of the indirect motivators: *emotional pressure*.

Emotional pressure suppresses performance and demotivates. It is connected to your self-perception. It arises when emotions like guilt, disappointment or shame—or external forces like the judgements you fear others may pass on you—drive you to do an activity. In a corporate environment, a lot of emotional pressure comes either from the individual's manager or from themselves: we can often be our own harshest critics and set unreasonable expectations for ourselves.

So, you might be doing a really great job but just don't see it. Or you constantly think things like, "I don't want to disappoint my manager/my team. I should know this. I shouldn't need to ask for help."

Reducing that emotional pressure on your direct reports provides a great boost to performance, but you can only remove that pressure if you first recognize that it is there. You can't just say, "I don't do any of those things. I don't guilt my people. I don't call them out or embarrass them. If I'm not doing that, I'm OK." It's not enough to simply not indulge in behaviours that overtly apply pressure: you have to work at actively mitigating the pressure. Just because you are not shaming them, doesn't mean they don't feel shame. So, you have to work to mitigate it; to make people feel safe.

This idea of emotional pressure is critical because, however logical and rational we may like to believe we are, people make decisions based on emotion, and then justify their decision with logic. Remember what I said about the three levels of the brain: the Reptile Brain casts its vote first, responding to fear. Then the Mammalian Brain gets to weigh in on the decision. Those are both driven by emotions. Finally, the Neo-cortex—the logical brain—joins in.

So, our plan is more likely to be based on emotion first: "I'm afraid that if I say this to my boss, they'll be angry, so I'd better write that instead," or, "I like this plan. I feel good about it." Then we create spreadsheets and slides and action plans to show how we are going to achieve whatever we are committing to. But when someone challenges our plan, we say "No, no, it's all based on perfect logic. Look at my beautiful annual plan. I have 500 pages of backup schedules!" We conveniently overlook that it started with a feeling.

It also factors into performance management. In most organizations, it is only the lowest grading that will result in a real loss for someone—many companies, for example, let go of their bottom 10% of performers as a matter of policy. And yet, people are terrified of getting anything other than the top grade. Why? Because of the shame—the emotional pressure, both internal and external—that goes with not being a "top performer."

Francis stared across the desk at me. "I can't believe I got a 4. A stinking FOUR! I feel like a failure. I feel like everyone is staring at me out there. Like they all KNOW."

Now bear in mind two things. First, no-one could know what his grade was. It wasn't something we shared with anyone other than the employee.

Second, four wasn't a bad grade. Admittedly, the scale we used covered 1-5, but it wasn't a linear scale. It was very top-heavy.

1 meant you were a superstar, while 2 meant "you are close to being a superstar." 3 meant "we really value you, you're a really good employee," and 4 meant, "you

> are still pretty good but you didn't hit it out of the park."
>
> In other words, 4 meant you'd done what we expected of you, and you had done it well, just not spectacularly. You were still a valued contributor.
>
> Did this person feel like a valued contributor?
>
> No! In fact, the most shocking thing was when Francis told me he felt "dirty": it's not a word I'd expected to hear from someone discussing their performance review. Other employees who received a 4 would say things like, "Why am I not good enough to be here?"
>
> There was so much shame and guilt in people's comments, it was alarming. And a 3 wasn't much better: people still saw it as a condemnation.

Another indirect motivator, according to Doshi and McGregor, is *Economic pressure*. This is about doing something to get a reward or avoid punishment. And if that sounds like traditional performance management, that's because it is: carrot and stick. And if the carrot isn't big enough, use a bigger stick.

In terms of our triangles, of course, economic pressure works purely on what is inside the Trust Box (Figure 13 on page 118): purpose and identity and values don't come into it. It's a case of, "If you do behaviour X or generate result X, you get a treat. If you don't do X, you get a penalty." Nowhere is that more apparent than in the grading approach that says that top-graded employees get a bonus and promotion—and maybe even an expenses-paid trip—while the bottom grade—as discussed above—get to discover what it's like working for a new employer.

That creates enormous amounts of internal competition, as we saw earlier, which reinforces the economic and emotional pressure.

In Maslow's terms, economic pressure is about safety and security, while emotional pressure is about losing relationships and self-esteem. The fear is that, while you may not die, you're going to be friendless, homeless, soulless and worthless.

How do you make people comfortable with adaptive performance?

So, how do we make people comfortable with adaptive performance? In other words, how do we make people comfortable with deviating from the plan?

First of all, you have to understand that managers often don't realize that these systems and structures that they are supporting are actually causing the damage.

> As I said earlier in this book, in 2016, Wells Fargo became mired in a mis-selling scandal. Employees had been pushing clients to buy products that weren't suitable for them just so they could hit targets. It's not that Wells Fargo leadership were standing over employees saying, "Ignore the clients' needs. Sell them the high-margin products." But internal reward mechanisms had been set up to encourage just that kind of behaviour. Employees were under intense economic and emotional pressure to break the rules.

Second, mitigate the emotional pressure I just spoke about by giving people permission to be themselves, to make mistakes, and to also recognize there are some areas where it is not good to make a mistake.

> In our team meetings, I would encourage people to talk about an unanticipated situation from the preceding week or a mistake that they had made, how they responded to it, and what they would do differently the next time. You had just three minutes to discuss it, so it wasn't about wallowing or making excuses—it was simply about the lesson learned.

Third, give examples from your own experience of how you have seen people overcome the pressures. In my one-on-ones and team meetings, I would go out of my way to find an example—either myself, a senior leader, or a peer of the person I was meeting—where there had been a release of the emotional pressure.

> One of my clients is a CEO who inadvertently put immense emotional pressure on her employees while trying to improve customer service! Seeing the havoc she was causing, she called everyone together for an all-hands meeting and apologized.
>
> In her earnest desire to help customers and deliver outstanding quality service, she had lost sight of the impact her dreams were having on the staff.
>
> She had allowed her "big vision" to obscure the details of implementation, and her staff was paying the price: overworked and constantly changing directions.
>
> And so she gave them permission to pull her back on track if she deviated like that ever again.

How do we get people to do what needs to be done?

Above, I discussed the *indirect* motivators and the powerful impact they can have on someone's ability to adapt. Doshi and McGregor discuss a further three factors, which they call *direct* motivators: Play, Purpose, and Potential.

Play is when you perform an activity simply because you enjoy it. The work itself is the reward. This is closely connected with the concept of "Flow" as described by Mihail Csikszentmihalyi[31]. When you are in flow, work stops feeling like work. Now, if you've ever watched a child playing, you know that there is also an aspect of play that is about curiosity, experimentation, and a willingness to let go of your fear. Confidence has a major part to play in this: when you are in play/flow, you are feeling good and confident, so you are willing to take more risks. That naturally makes people more adaptable and flexible: it encourages them to "try stuff and just see what happens."

Purpose refers to valuing the outcome of an activity. As we have seen, it is critical that you have some degree of alignment between the organization's purpose and the individual's purpose: the tips of the two pyramids need to be touching. When they *are* touching, it is a powerful motivator, and gives people confidence to deviate from the plan.

Potential refers to doing the work because you know it is going to lead to something important. For me personally, that was always a big driver.

---

[31] Csikszentmihalyi, Mihaly (1990). *Flow: The Psychology of Optimal Experience.* New York: Harper and Row

Tapping into that potential in yourself that you know you have takes us into the realms of self-actualization in Maslow terms. Which leads to an interesting observation: the *indirect* factors (emotional pressure and economic pressure) work up from the bottom needs, while the *direct* factors (purpose, play, and potential) work down from the top. We've seen that before. In effect, we're saying that transactional leaders rely on indirect motivation, while transformational leaders rely on direct motivation.

So what?

Ultimately, if you want people to be adaptable, you need to help them to be adaptable. That requires more trust: the bigger the trust box becomes, the more adaptable people can be.

WATCH THE VIDEOS

Want to learn more about the
Purposeful Workplace Experience?

Visit this site to watch me speak about it.

http://pinnacleculture.ca/bookvideos/

Summary

❖ Expect to deviate from your tactical plans but use the strategic plan to stay focused. Most times you are heading for the same outcome, you just have to change the way you're getting there.

❖ Scenario planning focuses on the content and responding directly to what happened, while adaptability focused on the context of the situation and rethinking on the path to get there.

❖ Using lead and lag indicators to track progress can help people embrace adaptability because it measures progress without waiting until the last minute.

❖ Emotional and economic pressure can block all efforts to be adaptable because they are based in fear of judgement.

❖ Generate confidence in individuals by focusing on their potential, helping them find purpose and allowing them to do what they love.

Chapter Twelve

The Rule of Equivalence: "Everyone can be a leader if you give them the opportunity"

In today's workplace, you need everyone to contribute at their fullest potential; there's no room for floaters anymore. While not everyone can have "manager" in their title, everyone does have the ability to lead, given the right conditions.

When Paul was diagnosed, I treated it as a management issue in many ways. Luckily, at that stage, we didn't have children who needed to be "protected" from the news. But we both had parents and friends, and I did my best to shield them. In reality, I was probably shielding myself even more. I remember telling one particular friend what was happening. She started to cry.

I said, "Stop it" and she just looked at me. "There's no need to cry, there doesn't need to be anything sad about this, so don't cry."

Years later, she asked me, "What were you thinking?"

I had no idea. I just knew that I didn't want people to feel sorry for us.

It's not easy telling parents their child is sick, even when that child is in his 30s. When we told them, Paul's mother began to wail. I couldn't take it. I had to leave the room.

Paul followed me out. "Paul, I can't do this," I said. "I can't watch your mother go through this."

He looked at me and put his hand on my shoulder. "I need you. I need you to be there."

Family members and friends all thought I didn't cry. That I never cried about what happened. I did. There were plenty of tears. They just never saw them.

I was trying to shield everybody, as though seeing me cry would make it harder for them. It was my management problem. I tried to take it on for them and protect them. And I did. I paid the price for my bravado. I worked myself into the ground and burnt out.

Interestingly, while I was running around trying to shield anyone and everyone from the pain, I never took that approach with our sons. I never tried to hide their father's illness from them. In part, that's because it was all they knew. They grew up making regular trips to the hospital and to Hearthplace. By the time Andrew was two and Ayden was three, they were already talking to psychologists.

The idea that daddy was dying was just part of life. We'd had conversations about what it meant to die, and the need to let emotions out rather than bottling them up. In reality, we were giving them the skills to be leaders.

Cancer hits the whole family: mother, father, daughter, son, wife, husband. Yes, the patient is at the centre of it. They get a lot of attention and focus, but there are a lot of unknown casualties around them.

VUCA is just the same. It hits everyone in the organization. A lot of attention can go to senior leaders or high-potential employees, but there can be a lot of casualties in other groups that go unnoticed.

The problem with how organizations have typically approached VUCA is that they have tended to treat it as a management issue. Usually, the senior management team tries to shelter the rest of the organization. The idea is that, while they deal with the volatility and external factors, everyone else can stay focused on the business. But, it's not just a leadership challenge, any more than it's just a customer service issue or a supply chain problem.

As I've already said, today's workplace is a network of teams, all trying to respond, predict and adapt. That's not easy to do, and in order to do it, we have to focus steadily on teamwork, on leveraging those networks, on keeping information open and out there and being very transparent.

And sometimes, VUCA doesn't hit the company directly. It can hit a stakeholder or multiple stakeholders. So you have to be ready for VUCA to hit both internally and externally. Look at what happened when the markets collapsed in 2009. Just because you weren't a bank, it didn't mean you were safe from the VUCA that was hitting the banks.

The result is, you can't treat VUCA as an interesting conundrum for the C-suite to ponder. The people on the ground or closest to the customers are often the best people to handle it. They are the ones in the trenches. In that respect, the standard corporate org chart is of very little use when VUCA hits. You have to lean into the network of teams.

To do that, we start by adopting an assumption that no team is necessarily "better" than any other and that hierarchical position has very little meaning in uncertain times. This is what I mean when I talk about *equivalence*.

It's not the same thing as *equality*: I'm not saying we need to treat everyone as equals. I'm not saying that we get rid of titles and pay differentials.

Monetary compensation needs to match levels of responsibility. When you are at the top, you are carrying a lot of responsibility, and you should be fairly compensated for that.

But in terms of where you can look for answers to get you through VUCA, you need to open your eyes and be much more open-minded than in the past.

Why organizations struggle

The key things that make it hard for organizations to deal with VUCA are short-term incentives and the org chart.

Short-term incentives are so deeply ingrained into our remuneration policies that it is hard to think of anything else. Structures and systems are built around it because most organizations are set up for short-term profit: you have to pay the shareholders, and leaders get very little credit—from their superiors, from the stock markets or from individual investors—for long-term vision. And, since few leaders actually end up staying in a role for the long-term, it's hard to see a long-term strategy ever bear fruit.

"Manager" is so 2010

In the brave new world of work, much of the traditional role of the manager is becoming—or, indeed, has already become—obsolete. There seems to be no limit to what can be automated. Technology is infiltrating and disrupting our workplaces. As a result, we don't need managers to do a lot of what we used to expect them to do: tasks that revolved around process and systems.

Indeed, it's not inconceivable that the role of a functional "manager' might one day disappear altogether.

Leaders, however, will always be needed: even if "management"—which is really about control and efficiency—can be automated, leadership cannot.

Leadership is about people working with people. It's about trust and authenticity and long term-perspective and that, I believe, technology will never take over.

Allowing everyone to step up and be a leader (but not necessarily a manager) will help organizations manage VUCA, and has the side benefit that it allows new leaders to emerge that traditional talent management systems would not have found.

Everyone is a leader

I'll say it again, in simple terms. Everyone is a leader. I don't mean that in an egalitarian, utopian "all must have prizes" kind of way. I simply mean that leadership is situational. Depending on what is happening, every individual in a team will have a critical role to play at some point. They will have unique input or skills or knowledge to bring to bear, and at that moment, they are the leader (even if it isn't reflected in their title or the org chart).

The skills that make leaders successful are different from the skills that make a manager successful. It's down to the ability to generate authentic conversations and build authentic relationships. It doesn't mean you need to be best friends with everyone, but you need a level of authenticity, trust, and empathy so people know you are being real. When you are being real, they will be real.

> *With the rise of the knowledge worker, one does not 'manage' people. The task is to lead people, and the goal is to make productive the specific strengths and knowledge of every individual.*—**Peter Drucker**

Timing matters

In most organizations, leadership training is given to someone when they have been identified as a potential leader, and they are being prepared for promotion in the near future. (Sometimes, the promotion may even come before the training!)

So, why is it a problem waiting until someone is in a management role—or at least being considered for one—before you give them leadership training?

Part of the problem is the millennials. They want to develop faster and earlier than other generations. If you apply the old mindset and tell them they will have to wait their turn, they will go somewhere else. They are putting pressure on the system.

You can't force learning to happen when you want it to, and you can't afford to sit around waiting for a neatly packaged, self-contained situation. Learning opportunities will arise every day, and you have to be ready to let people take advantage of them as they come along, to share their perspective and insight, and grow from that opportunity.

You can't push development and learning into a little box. It is going on around you all the time. So, are you going to leverage it and grow, or are you going to try to confine it and contain it to make it neat, predictable and stable?

The supreme irony is that many organizations—especially knowledge-based organizations—take the view that you have to display leadership and then you'll get promoted into a leadership position but, at the same time, they will only teach someone to lead once they are promoted.

You can still be a good leader, even if you don't have direct reports. The defining characteristic of a leader is the questions they ask.

Leaders tend to ask questions: *Why do you need these resources? Why are you behind plan? Why did you choose that course of action?* Managers, on the other hand, tend to instruct: *Get back on plan. Get this done. Improve productivity.*

One of the best leaders I've ever worked with wasn't a leader on paper, but she was a leader, nonetheless. Her leadership showed in the questions she asked and how she elevated the game of everyone around her. She asked 'why?' She had curiosity. She was always sharing different ideas. She believed in the people around her. And she was being authentic: she wasn't trying to manage a process or career, she just wanted to get things done and make a difference in a way that aligned to her own purpose and vision. For someone in her 20s, she had a very well-defined vision of what she wanted and the purpose she was looking for from any job she was given.

From ladders to jungle gyms

Organizations love scales and grades. They arrange people neatly, as though they were on a ladder. It gives everyone a high degree of certainty. When you put a ladder in front of somebody, they want to climb it, even if they don't know what's at the top.

If you show them what's at the top and say, "This is what you need to do to get to the next step," and when they get there, "Now do this to get to the next step," it becomes a great way of controlling their behaviour and making people toe the company line.

But what happens to that in an environment where there is total equivalence and a learning culture, and everybody is getting leadership opportunities?

The ladder turns into a jungle gym. It becomes a space that you explore, where you can crawl around and get a better perspective. And people love to explore.

Exploration gives you perspective. You can come at the "jungle gym" from different directions, and you can have multiple people on it at the same time, in different positions.

Some people are looking at their career more like a jungle gym than a ladder. It is not about the constant rise to the top; it's about *breadth* of experience as well as depth.

One of the first things you can do is to take a long, hard look at the titles you use in your organization. There are many alternatives to using the word "manager" everywhere: Chief Experience Officer; Division or Department Lead; Customer Lead instead of Customer Service Manager.

Of course, part of the appeal of management titles is that they give people certainty and security: they know where they fit in the hierarchy and they know what step they are on. A jungle gym is exciting, but it can also be scary!

There are also people who *need* those titles, and there's a risk they may leave if they can't get a formal "management" position. If they are valuable assets to the organization, that may be a risk you're not willing to take.

That's when you need to have a deep conversation as a leadership team about what are you trying to do. Are you looking for a short-term gain, or trying to drive long-term culture change? What are you trying to build? What will the impact be if technically capable people leave because you are renaming positions? Are those people the kind you necessarily want to keep? What are they like from a behavioural perspective? Will the short-term pain for their team of losing them be outweighed by the long-term gains across the whole company?

You need to evolve your mindset—and I appreciate that this is a big change to make—but at the very least, even if you can't change titles, you can make other changes around you.

Help managers to build leadership skills that expand accountability across their team. Reward them for investing time in their team members' growth and development. Create a leadership team focused on organizational decisions rather than their narrow departmental silos.

> At one of my clients, we've taken what was a loose group of managers talking about actions, controls, and efficiency and turned them into leaders who are making decisions not just for their own department, but for the organization as a whole. They are being rebranded as the Leadership Team, and we are bringing them together to define what their role is and how they are going to lead the organization, not just their department. Rather than taking them out of their day job for a lengthy retreat, however, we are doing it in bite-size chunks during their regular meetings.

Create Equivalence

Treating everyone as potential equals creates an environment of what I call "equivalence" in which titles are replaced with terms that are less nuanced.

As organizations become flatter, the title of leadership becomes less attainable. In most organizations, there are fewer middle managers and therefore fewer opportunities for individual contributors to be promoted to management roles. And when they do become managers, they are sandwiched in the middle, between their direct reports and the leadership of the organization. They have leadership responsibilities, but they also have responsibilities for delivery.

Organizations like Microsoft have tried to reduce that pressure by creating separate career tracks for people who want to focus specifically on delivery and those who want to take on people management responsibilities. It's a way of ensuring the company can accommodate people who are technically brilliant but who you might not want to put in charge of other people. The technical track allows specialists to rise through the organizational hierarchy in the same way as people managers, but with their own set of titles. Even though the titles and grades are directly equivalent, and carry similar pay and rewards, however, people on the technical track feel under immense emotional pressure (most of it of their own creation) to move into the people management track so they can get a title that says "manager". People want to climb the ladder, even though they are being told they don't have to.

Stacking the triangles

Equivalence contributes to keeping the triangles aligned. It does that by encouraging employees to identify more closely with the organization than with the career path. Once you strip the career path out, they are no longer climbing that ladder: they are exploring the jungle gym. So, with the ladder, the loyalty is to the career progression, and a lot of people will jump ship simply to get to the next stage in their career. *"I can join that organization over there because that means I'll have the title of senior manager, which I'm not getting here. So I'll go over there, and I've moved forward in my career."*

If the titles and rigmarole aren't there, what you are saying to somebody is "Look, here is an organization where you can do virtually whatever you like. You can go and explore any part of the organization. Here, you'll be able to build your career how you want it." So, when they are ready for the next stage, it's a question of what's next on the jungle gym?

It works because, when you align the two triangles, you are aligning the individual's identity with the organization rather than the job title. So you have a community of people who are invested in the values, who understand that their values and beliefs and the organization's values and beliefs are aligned.

And when you have that, you can weather the storm with much more grace and success.

When you look at the triangles, the base is a lot wider, broader and more substantial than the little triangle at the top. So that sense of purpose, identity, and values and beliefs provides a far more stable foundation than behaviours.

Equivalence is scary

The concept of equivalence challenges our need for self-esteem and significance. It also challenges the psychological safety for managers and employees, because you're removing from their life the certainty that the typical career ladder provides.

In exchange, they get to strengthen their sense of belonging and self-actualization.

For an employee, their big fear is that they no longer understand where they fit in the organization. They are being asked to act like a leader—sometimes for the first time in their career—and they may be on unfamiliar ground. They worry that they'll be held accountable and that their work-load is about to expand.

So, it's critical that you make them feel safe and supported. That requires expanding the trust box—as so much in the Purposeful Workplace Experience™ does. You may have to challenge some long-held beliefs and values, through one-to-one coaching as well as collectively.

In some organizations, that one-to-one coaching has been taken down to all levels of the company through on-demand coaching programs. In others, with a more restricted budget, individual coaching may have to be reserved for leaders and High Potentials, at least initially, in which case a major focus of that program has to be to give those individuals the skills they need to have similar conversations with their own direct reports.

The power of authenticity

Equivalence depends, to a great degree, on expanding the trust box, and we've already discussed the importance of trust as a way of lowering the "water line" on our triangles.

Trust can only happen when you deal with your direct reports authentically. Now, authenticity is a word that gets thrown around a lot in leadership training and books, but what does it really mean?

Saying that it's about being "real" or "open" isn't particularly helpful—I'm sure we could all figure out that being "real" makes you "authentic". So, let's dive a little deeper.

Authenticity depends on five characteristics.

- Authentic leaders have the ability to take on board and process information about themselves and adjust their leadership style accordingly.
- They also make adjustments as circumstances and the environment change.
- Their sense of personal identity is strong enough, and grounded enough in who they are—the base of their triangle—that they can make adjustments without feeling that they are somehow "losing themselves". That's important because it's what allows them to align their pyramid with the organization's pyramid.
- If the organization's pyramid shifts, they know how to shift with it.
- Authentic leaders are also strong enough in their sense of identity that they're not afraid to show it at work.

Authenticity also means taking responsibility for your own experiences—be they thoughts, emotions, needs, preferences or beliefs—rather than trying to hide them or diminish them. Thinking about that in terms of our triangles, it means understanding how what's under the water line has created what is above the water line.

Along with those behaviours, we find two other key traits in Authentic Leadership Theory[32] that resonate deeply with

[32] Černe, M., Dimovski, V., Mari, M., Penger, S., & Kerlavaj, M. (2014). Congruence of leader self-perceptions and follower perceptions of authentic leadership: Understanding what authentic leadership is and

leaders who have implemented a Purposeful Workplace Experience™.

First is self-awareness. Why is the authentic leader so receptive to feedback? Because they know themselves well enough to know when that feedback is true.

Second is "balanced processing": the ability to analyze a situation objectively, and with as little bias as possible before making a decision. Again, the language there is important. Bias is going to happen. You'd have to be inhuman to set all bias aside. So, I'm not saying that an authentic leader is some sort of superhero, simply that they know their biases, and they do their best to keep them out of the decision-making process. And, yes, once again, it's about understanding your triangle and what is below the surface.

So, an authentic leader knows their triangle, knows how it has been constructed, keeps it aligned at all times, and they don't feel the need to hide it.

There's a major difference between "toeing the company line" and aligning yourself with the organization: an authentic leader brings themselves into line *because* it fits with who they are; an inauthentic leader brings themselves into line with the organization even though it's at odds with who they truly are. So, an inauthentic leader doesn't feel they can be themselves at work because people would notice the difference.

---

how it enhances employees' job satisfaction. Australian Journal of Management, 39(3), 453-471.

That is also one of the key differentiators between this idea of authentic leadership[33] and theories like transformational leadership: other theories often describe what you have to do without considering whether that is being true to yourself.

> When we were doing performance reviews, our HR business partner would ask questions to ensure that the evidence we were using to support our ratings was consistent across everybody who shared a ranking of that level. For example, they went out of their way to eliminate recency bias—where too much emphasis is given to performance in the latest months, and things that happened earlier in the period are neglected.

Third, authentic leaders are open and transparent in their relationship with co-workers. Notice that I'm not saying that authenticity means constantly sharing who you are. It's not about constantly talking about your beliefs and values, your purpose, or anything like that. It's simply that,

1. When the situation calls for it, you don't feel the need to hide those things.

2. You are comfortable enough in your own skin to take feedback and adjust.

3. You never give in to the temptation to behave out of alignment.

---

[33] Walumbwa, F. O., Avolio, B. J., Gardner, W. L., Wernsing, T. S., & Peterson, S. J. (2008, February). Authentic Leadership: Development and Validation of a Theory-Based Measure. Journal of Management, 34(1), 89-126.

In effect, the authentic leader is one who takes the whole triangle with them and doesn't just keep shifting the top around.

A VP I worked with received feedback that they could come across as too intense. It was the first time they had ever had that feedback, and it was from somebody whom they didn't know but whose judgement they respected.

The comment got this VP thinking, and they asked me whether I'd ever noticed it. So I gave some examples of times when I thought they might have given that impression to people, and they took them away to reflect on them.

A few weeks later, this leader came back to me. "I've really been thinking about this. I looked at these examples, and now I think I see where that feedback might be coming from."

This story is a perfect example of taking ownership of behaviours and experience, and saying *"OK. If I'm being told this, there is something I've done to create it. This person isn't making it up to make me feel bad."* Instead, the VP sought to understand what was behind the feedback—it turned out to be a behaviour that only came out with certain types of people, in certain situations.

Being authentic can be scary too

Managers have a number of fears around being authentic. We are not, as a culture, encouraged—or accustomed—to being vulnerable. We are not used to seeing people at the top admit that they have made a mistake. It's scary, making a stand while knowing that people are going to judge you.

If you also think of traditional ideas of "leadership"—strong and decisive; grit and determination in the face of adversity—showing vulnerability can feel like a loss of face, and therefore of significance, which impacts self-esteem.

And so, it can be hard to start being authentic, especially if you've always put up a façade. But the relational transparency and self-awareness that go with authenticity create an environment of trust and honesty, which in turn make it easier for your direct reports to be engaged, both with you and with the organization. It also makes you an effective organizational leader, even when it's not in your title.

One of the main differences that set authentic leaders apart from leaders who are "merely" transformational, is the ethical and moral basis underpinning what they do: authentic leaders are grounded by the lower part of their triangle— their purpose, identity, values, and beliefs. I believe that is more important than ever in today's day and age because there are no right or wrong answers, so you absolutely have to have that strong moral compass.

Authenticity and influence

The influence of authentic leaders is not about transforming followers to their desires. Rather, it represents a more engaged, positive, self-development of the followers. In effect, an authentic leader will help that individual to build out the base of their pyramid and expand the Trust Box so that everyone—leader and employees alike—feels able to be more open and communicate more authentically.

That creates an environment that encourages debate and healthy conflict, invites diverse viewpoints, and fosters better, faster decisions in the face of VUCA regardless of your formal job title.

WATCH THE VIDEOS

Want to learn more about the
Purposeful Workplace Experience?

Visit this site to watch me speak about it.

http://pinnacleculture.ca/bookvideos/

Summary

❖ VUCA will impact every level of your organization and employees can't be protected from it but that's ok because the answers a company needs when responding to it lie at all levels anyway. This is the concept of equivalence in finding solutions for customers.

❖ Leaders build authentic relationships and generate conversations instead of managing or directing answers. You don't need a formal title to be a leader.

❖ Think of your career as a jungle gym instead of a ladder. There's value in depth of experience and taking your time to explore. Besides, there's way more room to play on a jungle gym and there's no race to the top. Frankly, it can be quite lonely up there anyway.

❖ Authenticity depends on five characteristics: (1) processes info about themselves and adjusts their style accordingly, (2) makes adjustments as circumstances in the environment change, (3) have a grounded sense of identity, (4) receptive to feedback due to their strong self-awareness and (5) objectively analyze a situation and reduce bias as much as possible

❖ Authentic leaders create an environment of trust and honesty, making employees feel safe and willing to contribute, especially during turbulent times.

Conclusion

It's easy to measure *what* is being done. It's much harder to measure *how* it gets done. "How" is so intangible that it's much easier to simply ignore it or deny its existence.

In the world of VUCA, that attitude won't work anymore. You need to understand what is happening under the surface, behind the Trust Boundary. You need to understand what makes your employees tick, just as you need to understand what makes the organization itself tick as well.

That is all that stands between you and failure.

When Paul was first diagnosed, I was 32 years old. Two years into his illness, I had two infants and a husband who, given the disease that was eating away at his body, should have already been dead.

By rights, I should have been consumed by fear. But I wasn't. Nor was I obsessing over what others thought about me at work. I was still delivering high-quality work: indeed, I was promoted three times during his illness.

I was living—and working—by my own values, I was acting with integrity, and my authentic self was shining through and guiding my behaviour.

I just happened to have this other "situation" going on, and in my mind, I simply didn't have time to worry about "needless stuff." I was focusing all my energy and time on things that really mattered.

Every one of us has a story. Mine isn't any more special than yours. You can let it define you or you can define how it will make you.   It is because of my story, personally and professionally, that I created the Purposeful Workplace Experience. I chose to define what this story would make me.   I learned about the power of permission and fear and the beauty of authenticity and purpose – in my personal life and in the workplace.

Being widowed at a young age with two young boys was a painful experience but it was a powerful leadership lesson. I learned about the power of connecting to a person, not a process. I found comfort and strength collaborating with other families facing a terminal illness of a loved one. I learned how to adapt a family plan and live CT scan to CT scan without losing track of the end goal to be a happy, nurturing family. And finally, I learned that playing on a jungle gym instead of trying to race up a ladder is much more fulfilling.

As our world speeds up, we need to slow down. We need to be thoughtful with our own purpose and allow ourselves to connect with each other. Our workplaces are being disrupted and in the effort to keep up and outperform, we continue to be chronically underproductive.

I believe there is a vast amount of potential to be unleashed taking companies to an entirely new level of productivity. We just need to look at it through a different lens. The

Purposeful Workplace Experience™ is part of this new perspective.

My hope is that this book has given you a new framework to understand how to power your business. Your company strategy may be brilliant, but it won't be implemented well by individuals who are overwhelmed and disconnected. Don't fall into the trap of thinking your teams are fine and you don't have anything to worry about. The chances are you have many employees, including the high-potentials, who are searching for more meaning, development and inspiration. Do you understand their perspective or are you resting on your laurels?

We need leaders who aren't afraid, who mitigate fear, who don't require permission but instead connect with people in authentic ways and build trust. Leaders who can manage the ambiguity and be confident in their decisions. Leaders who see the workplace as an experience that helps people to grow and not a place where transactions and tasks are performed.

Purposeful Workplace Experience™ is more than Coaching

Traditionally, organizations have used coaching to support the individual, either to help them bring their values and beliefs into line with the organization, or help them to exit if they can't.

Just as change consultants tend to focus only on the organization and ignore the individual, coaches work solely on the individual: they are not there to change the company.

Purposeful Workplace Experience™ crosses that divide. It's about measuring the beliefs and values of both the individual and the organization. It's about recognizing that the bottom of the triangle does exist and realigning it. It's not about tearing everything apart; it's about creating the realignment in a minimally disruptive way, while at the same time dealing with VUCA.

The Power of Permission

I would like to share one final story. I see it as a metaphor for the challenges we all face in the workplace. Whether your leadership role is formal or informal, recognize how powerful permission can be. Our workforce is overwhelmed and trying to cope with challenging circumstances every day. Simply giving people permission to be human can unleash powerful outcomes.

> January 2009. Paul had been ill for just short of six years.
>
> A month before, in mid-December, he had been hospitalized, and we thought that this was it. He had gone downhill quickly. He was in a lot of pain, and we had nurses coming in. I started to prepare the boys for what was coming.
>
> Because it was so close to the holidays, we were offered the option of a blood transfusion that would give him another few weeks of life. It meant we got one final Christmas together as a family—not the most enjoyable Christmas, but at least we had it together.
>
> Within a few weeks—the middle of January—the pain became intolerable, and his hallucinations got worse.

I was at a sales conference in New York when my phone rang. It was my mom. "We had to take Paul to the hospital."

I got the first flight home. By the time I got to the hospital, they had him in a room, and he was in agony.

With his family by his side, and a priest to give him the Last Rites, he wasn't expected to make it past the next 48 hours. Two days later they had managed to get the pain under control, and he started doing better. He even managed to eat a little. He was interacting with people—not in depth, but he was interacting—and he ended up making it through the whole weekend.

We were all shocked. Paul just kept going—he was like the Energizer Bunny. The truth is my Paul—the Paul I knew; the Paul I had married—had passed away eighteen months before. What was in the hospital bed was just the physical shell, and it was suffering.

On Monday morning, the palliative care doctor came in and said, "Your husband has had a really good weekend."

"I know," I said.

The doctor continued. "One of two things is going to happen in the next few days. Either he is going to pass away, and this was just the last burst of energy before passing, or we are going to have to send him home." I said "What?"

She said, "Well, this is a Palliative Care Unit, and if he starts getting better, we have to send him home."

Once she had left, I sat Paul up on the bed. I said, "You know who I am, right?" and he replied, "Yeah, you're my mom." Even in that moment, he managed a joke.

He smiled at me, to make sure I knew he wasn't serious, and I continued. "Paul, you know how much I love you, but this has been a long battle. You can't do this anymore. Our kids need two parents, and if you come home again, it's going to kill me." I squeezed his hand. "I can't do this anymore. I can't look after both you and the boys. It's OK for you to go now. We'll be OK."

He looked straight into my eyes. "I know. I'm trying."

At that moment, I realized that he needed to hear from me that we were going to be OK.

I had given him permission, and just a few hours later the convulsions started, and they had to medicate him. He spent the next 24 hours sedated and never woke up. He passed peacefully with no pain and surrounded by those who loved him.

That was such a strong lesson for me about the power of permission. Here was this strong man, who we clearly didn't want to go, but it had been such a long battle. When I finally did give him that permission, I believe he let go of the fear and left peacefully.

Will You Leave a Book Review?

Did you enjoy this book? Did you find it useful? If you did, I'd be grateful if you post a short review!

Your support makes a real difference. I read all reviews personally, and use them to make this book even better

To leave a review right now on Amazon, go here:
www.PinnacleCulture.ca/ROE-Review

Made in the USA
San Bernardino,
CA